The Sound Bite Society

How Television Helps the Right and Hurts the Left

Jeffrey Scheuer

Routledge
New York and London

Published in 2001 by
Routledge
29 West 35th Street
New York, NY 10001

Published in Great Britain by
Routledge
11 New Fetter Lane
London EC4P 4EE

Routledge is an imprint of the Taylor and Francis Group.

Originally published in hardcover by Four Walls Eight Windows as
The Sound Bite Society: Television and the American Mind. This
paperback edition published by arrangement with Four Walls Eight
Windows.

Library of Congress Cataloging-in-Publication Data
Scheuer, Jeffrey, 1953–
   The sound bite society : how television helps the right and hurts
the left / Jeffrey Scheuer.
      p. cm.
   ISBN 0-41593662-4
   Includes bibliographical references and index.
      1. Television in politics–United States. 2. Television broadcast-
ing–United States. 3. Conservatism--United States. 4. United
States–Politics and government–1981–1989. 5. United
States–Politics and government–1989– I. Title

HE8700.76.U6 S34 2001
302.23'45'0973–dc21

                                                2001019755

Time makes old formulas look strange,
Our properties and symbols change,
But round the freedom of the Will
Our disagreements centre still,
And now as then the voter hears
The battle cries of two ideas.

—W. H. Auden,
"A New Year Letter"

For Winnie and Jeremy, who waited.

Contents

Acknowledgments

I am deeply indebted to many critics and scholars who have written insightfully on politics and the media, some of whom are listed in the selected bibliography. Along with the necessary conceit that I have something to add to their conversation, writing this book has made me humble and grateful to stand in their shadows.

In addition, the help, advice, and criticism of many people has contributed to this volume. For adding to its merits, I thank them; for its flaws I absolve them, including the distinguished circle who mainly found fault. I want to thank my unusually gifted editor, JillEllyn Riley; my wise and loyal agent, Mary Evans; my able research assistant, Gail Harper; and my trusted *consiglieri*, Mitchell Cohen, Richard Osterweil (who played a crucial role in the genesis of this book), Mark D. Schwartz, and Richard Sclove. For close readings of early drafts or chapters, I also want to thank Michael Bergmann, Nancy Kranich, Michael Massing, Victor Navasky, Ann Brownell Sloane, Michael Walzer, and

Marie Winn. Without each of them, this book would have been appreciably less than it is.

For further valuable insights in conversation and correspondence, I'd like to thank Philip E. Agre, Maud Anderson, Alfred H. Bloom, Michael S. Dukakis, Amy Edelman, Barbara Esgalhado, Stanley Fish, Herbert J. Gans, Todd Gitlin, Lawrence K. Grossman, the late Irving Howe, Nathan Kingsley, Stefan McKeown and Ilene Sterns, Hans Oberdiek, Brian Rose, and Matthew Rothschild.

My special personal thanks go to Ruth Scheuer for her support and cooperation; to Hattie Dixon; to Sam, Rachel, Daniella, Abigail, and Noah; and to my parents, Walter and Marge Scheuer, who made everything possible.

The Politics of Electronic Information

■

We've got to face it. Politics have entered a new stage, the television stage. Instead of long-winded public debates, the people want capsule slogans—"Time for a change"—"The mess in Washington"—"More bang for a buck"—punchlines and glamour.

—General Haynesworth, the media mogul in the
Budd Schulberg film *A Face in the Crowd*, 1957

1 · *The Sound Bite Society*

Two great trends, among and perhaps above others, have shaped American politics over the past generation. Their relationship, if recognized at all, is seldom clearly understood. One has been the emergence of television, not just as an important element in the political process, but as its very framework. The other is the nearly complete collapse of American liberalism in the face of a resurgent New Right, beginning with the election of Ronald Reagan in 1980 and continuing with the Republican takeover in the congressional elections of 1994 and subsequent conservative gains. These trends are connected, and the shaping of information by television affects the organization of political beliefs.

Needless to say, television is the dominant medium of a media-dominated age. Like the atom bomb, it arrived at midcentury and spawned intractable questions about technology and human values. Nuclear fission altered the nature of world power; television has likewise altered the nature of power but has had far greater impact on everyday life. Television doesn't just affect society; to a great extent, it *is* society. All politics is no longer simply local; most politics—and most popular culture—is televisual.

It is proverbial that knowledge is power, but until quite recently, this was only a limited truth in human affairs. For millennia, power on the larger scale has been sustained by other means: brute force; economic hegemony through the control of land or resources; recognized claims to rule and privilege based on tradition, divine authority, tribal law, or hereditary nobility; or, as so often in the past century, artful combinations of force and terror. Yet an astonishing reversal has occurred in the last half-century. As the Cold War ultimately proved, power in the modern era is often depleted by expansion and conquest, squandered by military adventurism. Military force itself is more information-intensive, involving high-tech surveillance and processing, situational awareness, and precision weaponry. "Soft power" based on perceptions and persuasion is offsetting force; an "information umbrella" is supplanting the nuclear umbrella of the Cold War era.[1] It is increasingly clear that power is ultimately linked to economic prosperity, and prosperity to information.

In a broader sense, the Information Age began with the printing press and the rise of mercantile capitalism, with its need for the registration of contracts and charters, banking and market information, and the like. But we now live in an era of instant and abundant electronic information, both textual and visual, driving an increasingly integrated world economy. For both the individual and the state, in the twenty-first century, the hard currency of power is knowledge. It therefore behooves democratic citizens to explore the connections between knowledge and power, and more specifically, between television, as the dominant mode of communication, and political power and ideas.

The Sound Bite Society aims to understand television, not to bash it. But it does not pretend that a culture driven by sound bites does not impoverish political debate. The outward symptoms of that impoverishment are everywhere: mindless and manipulative political advertising; shallow political dialogue and equally shallow TV news programs; a wide (but not always informed) mistrust of both media and political figures and institutions; electoral turnout below half of all eligible voters. The American media's treatment of the Clinton scandal has reflected the recession of serious news before the sensational; but while the salacious details of the Starr Report were natural grist for the sound bite mill, that mill and the political culture it spawned long predated President Clinton's misadventures and the partisan effort to impeach him.

Americans are capable of better things, and better leadership; but in a sound bite society, we cannot educate our children to the standard that a great and complex democracy deserves. In a sound bite society, the cash registers at fast-food restaurants have pictures of food items instead of numerals. Those pictures of burgers and fries really spell a dead-end to the American dream of a mobile, inclusive middle-class society and a vital democracy of engaged citizens. Our popular and political cultures are dominated by money and profit, imagery and spin, hype and personality—and there can be no doubt that the chief culprit is commercial television.

2 · *Technology and the Information Evolution*

As revolutionary as it was in midcentury, television is also part of a more gradual and continuing evolutionary progression: a link in the chain of communications technologies tracing to the advent of movable type. At least two key phases in that process were pre-electronic. First, the invention of the compound lens in the early seventeenth century allowed humankind to see itself in relation to both the macrocosmos and the microcosmos, via telescopes and microscopes respectively. Repositioning the human eye and mind in the universe, the lens spurred modern science and greatly influenced the course of art and culture as well.

A second phase, an inevitable result of the first despite a lag of two centuries, was the emergence of photography, leading to the mass dissemination of visual images. Morse's invention of the telegraph in 1844 initiated the electronic phase; but that too was only a link in the longer chain, followed by telephony, silent film, tape and phonograph recording, radio, and sound film. TV, with its multiple transmission capacities—live and recorded images, still and moving, sound and color—effectively completes a logical progression, collapsing the barriers of space and time. By simulating face-to-face human communication, it affords a level of proximity to remote experience that is a quantum leap beyond all prior modes.

As we enter a new millennium, important advances in telecommunications are imminent. Interactive TV is hard upon us, along with digital transmission, high definition, and the convergence of the TV and computer. Yet it's hard to foresee how future developments might comparably transform daily life, or fundamentally rearrange how we think and behave; and those would seem reasonable criteria for using the term 'revolution.' Important as they will be, it seems doubtful that further advances will allow us to travel in time, be in two or more places at once, or enter the minds of others. We are witnessing a revolution in the storage and delivery of information, as the point of delivery becomes more accessible, consolidated, miniaturized, and choice-enriched. But in the realm of communication—as compared to, say, transportation or medicine—the most obvious barriers have already fallen.

The advent of cyberspace—the likely arena of future television—is indeed revolutionary. But it is less an information goldmine than a plenitude of (often dubious) mine shafts. The Internet does not offer new information, but new ways of storing and moving it. Dazzling as this new frontier is, we need to remind ourselves that facts, ideas, and arguments are human constructs. Information is not some sort of manna, but a social product: human thought and observation encoded for communication. It is not some invaluable or inexhaustible mineral waiting to be extracted in proportion to available technology. Machines don't generate new information or even, in most cases, enrich the ore; they merely store, process, and transmit it from one human mind to another.

Moreover, few technologies are morally and politically innocuous, or purely neutral extensions of human capabilities. Often their effects are latent, obscure, unpredictable, or perverse. Gunpowder brought warfare to the masses, and the cotton gin prolonged slavery; modern transportation has made the world smaller at a cost of millions of lives; new weapons continue to expedite human slaughter, even as medical breakthroughs have expanded and complicated society's moral choices. While all technologies empower someone, they may empower the few to harm, exploit, or dominate the many. Anyone who thinks technology as such will bring harmony to the world is innocent of the unprecedented misery and mortality it has made possible in the disastrous century now ending.

Television, though seldom directly fatal, has particularly complicated and ambivalent social functions. The medium's most obvious shortcomings are well-known, and we needn't belabor them. Commercial TV at once epitomizes and amplifies everything mediocre and excessive in a consumer society. It manipulates our emotions, numbs us with social stereotypes, saturates us with the trivial and the superficial. It is both a wunderkind of twentieth-century technology (like the computer), with vast potential to inform and entertain, and a whore of profit.

These two technologies are about to merge, and the main features of this heralded "communications revolution" appear to be fourfold: aesthetics, convenience, choice, and interactivity. First, digital, high-definition TV will improve audiovisual fidelity. But this is no more revolutionary than, say, the advent of color TV or of compact and DVD disks. It is rather a welcome aesthetic enhancement.[2] A second benefit of the telecomputer (aside from consolidating household furniture) will be data on demand: a new level of consumer choice and convenience in terms of accessing, scheduling, and manipulating the information stream. The home entertainment center will likely merge the existing capacities of computers, film, television, videocassettes, and perhaps an indefinitely large audiovisual library. No more trips to the video store, only to be told by a salesperson who has never heard of Humphrey Bogart that *Casablanca* is unavailable; Sam will always be downloadable to "play it again." While it would be foolish to minimize the importance of this convergence, it's far from clear that the content of programming, or the essential character of the viewing experience, will be drastically altered.

Interactivity, which is already a feature of computer and video games, is indeed different from passive viewing, involving some control (or at least selectivity) of program content—even if it is more "inter" than "active." But the exact nature of interactivity remains unclear; and it is likewise unclear whether interactivity can yield more than an expanded menu of choices, or a vehicle for advertisers to customize their pitch to your personal consumption habits. Will viewers seeking more passive entertainment grow bored with hypertext and optional plot scenarios? Will a 300- or 500-channel system support the requisite creative talent to fill the digital pipeline, or will that pipeline gush with old movies and vintage episodes of *Seinfeld* and *The Honeymooners*? And is it not ironic that, after a half-century of trancelike TV viewing, we identify clicking a mouse to register choices as a form of "activity" at all?

The digital spectrum, interactive television, and data-on-demand portend an array of new entertainment vehicles and concierge services—such as games, movies and TV programs, educational programming, e-mail, interactive banking, home shopping, voting, polling, video conferencing, and telephone service—most of which are available through existing technologies. Their convergence represents a convenience revolution, more than a communications revolution. It will be a sure boon to shut-ins, hospital patients, and prisoners. It may also further isolate the rest of us, to the detriment of community and democratic life. As Ken Auletta, an astute media critic, observes, "The good news is that this video democracy will empower citizens to choose what they want, when they want it. The bad news is that people may read less. Perhaps more Americans will shutter themselves indoors to watch TV, avoiding social intercourse. There may be more me, less we."[3]

The Internet is an intriguing frontier, but it won't raise the kids or walk the dog. It may well subsume and alter TV, but it won't replace TV. We will still need to be informed and entertained via audiovisual programming; and the human brain will remain the most important and upgradable software we have. In short, TV, or something very much like it, will persist. If that prediction is wrong, and TV is about to give way to something unrecognizably different, then this book may merely shed some archeological light on the dominant global medium of the last half-century, and its relation to the politics of that era. But don't throw your set away just yet.

3 · *A Preview of the Argument*

A sound bite society is one that is flooded with images and slogans, bits of information and abbreviated or symbolic messages — a culture of instant but shallow communication. It is not just a culture of gratification and consumption, but one of immediacy and superficiality, in which the very notion of "news" erodes in a tide of formulaic mass entertainment. It is a society anesthetized to violence, one that is cynical but uncritical, and indifferent to, if not contemptuous of, the more complex human tasks of cooperation, conceptualization, and serious discourse.

Television is a primary agent of that process. But this book is not a catalogue of complaints about modernity, or a critique of television as a vehicle of intellectual, moral, or spiritual decay. There are enough good studies of the nature, content, and social impact of television.[4] However, there is an inferential connection between a sound bite society and a political ideology that emphasizes simple, boundary-oriented values: the self and the private, the mechanical and the obvious, the anonymous marketplace.

Narcissism and escapism are hardly recipes for social awareness or public enterprise.

In this book we will explore the bases and implications of that inference. We will not examine the content of television, or what this season's ratings reflect about our national tastes, or how TV socializes us or shapes specific (and important) issues such as race, gender, sexuality, faith, or parenting. The purpose is rather to relate television more generally to the core values and assumptions that underlie our political ideas. It is addressed to viewers across the political spectrum, to those who venerate as well as those who abhor the medium, and the many in between who claim only to watch *Seinfeld* reruns, classic movies, or Charlie Rose. Television is a marvel, but not a cornucopia; a cultural incubus, but not a malevolent engine of stupefaction, exerting irresistible stimulus-response effects on a wholly passive or homogenous audience. It can be a unique window on human experience, and it can put brains to bed. It can be a great boon to democratic life, and a great detriment. And its electronic footprint is all over our political ideas.

Television has altered the channels of power and political legitimation, and the very language of political discourse: an audio-visual vocabulary of images, slogans, and sound bites dominates political conversation. Because of this language, television favors certain political ideas and disfavors others. The electronic culture fragments information into isolated, dramatic particles and resists longer and more complex messages. These characteristics militate against a vision that emphasizes 1) change, including gradual or evolutionary change; 2) abstraction, an important tool for envisioning and framing change; 3) ambiguity and nonbinary thinking; 4) reasoning that appeals to causal, contextual, or environmental considerations; 5) divergence between appearance and reality; and 6) stronger bonds between individual, community, and nation. The sound bite culture in fact reinforces a contrary vision: one that focuses on the immediate and the obvious; the near-term, and the particular; on identity between appearance and reality; and on the self rather than larger communities. Above all, it is a society that thrives on simplicity and disdains complexity. And simplicity, I will suggest, is epitomically conservative, whereas complexity is quintessentially progressive.

The argument of this book, then, has two hinged parts, which form the twin premises of a broad, nondeductive syllogism. The first is that television, in nearly all its forms and functions, and for both economic and structural reasons, acts as a simplifying lens, filtering out complex ideas in favor of blunt emotional messages that appeal to the self and to narrower moral-political impulses. The second is that, for reasons that are inherent in the nature of ideology and do not impugn the politics of the left or right, simplification promotes, and epitomizes, political conservatism. Indeed, I will argue that simplicity and complexity are the basic polar organizing principles of the political spectrum. They explain not only our ideological differences (and why they are ultimately irreconcilable) but also why television is a potent vehicle of conservative messages and values and a concomitant brake on liberalism: why its increasing dominance of our political culture has been a central factor in the resurgence of American conservatism.

This is not to say that more complex theories or ideologies are better than simpler ones *a fortiori*. "Simpler" here emphatically does not mean simplistic or simpleminded. A simpler theory of government and the social contract is one that demands less of individuals and offers less in return; that argues for smaller government, lower taxes, fewer services, and less regulation, preferring to leave the market alone rather than to curb or offset it; that seeks to maximize personal autonomy over other freedoms, and implies that government—not other institutions or individuals—is the primary threat to individual freedom. A simpler ideology propounds a more rudimentary form of personal freedom (as opposed to one that offers greater protection from other individuals and institutions) and less equality.

The simplicity I ascribe to conservative values and messages is, at least in a tactical sense, an important source of their appeal—and a reason why they play so well on the airwaves. But the twin claims that television simplifies and that simplicity abets conservatism are not partisan ones. The arguments of the left and the right may be equally sophisticated or flawed. *It is not the arguments or strategies but the underlying values and visions that are simpler and more complex, respectively.* And those core values of simplicity and complexity cannot be peremptorily disqualified.

A measure of agnosticism, therefore, is not only compatible with fervent ideological commitment, but necessary for a truly democratic climate of debate. A mature democracy not only tolerates but demands respectful discourse across a broad range of responsible opinion. It recognizes the validity and the essential dignity of progressive and conservative ideas alike, and comprehends why these polar tendencies persist in defining our political arguments—even in an anti-ideological (not to say anti-intellectual) culture. Such respectful discourse is precisely what television does not deliver for American democracy at present.

Television's simplifying bias is not conscious, insidious, or unfair. To be sure, TV may militate against the public sphere in other ways, for example in its commercialism—thus obscuring or denigrating less profit-driven or self-regarding activities such as nonprofit enterprise, activism, voluntarism, philanthropy, public service, and nonconsumerist avocations. But the simpler vision, like the more complex one, is inherently respectable, even if television—and politicians on television—do not always purvey it in a respectable form.

Similarly, liberalism is uniquely challenged in a television-saturated society; but to say that liberalism (or conservatism for that matter) is outdated or defunct is a willful misconception, a cheap polemical thrust. Political tides ebb and flow; issues and tactics change and adapt to new circumstances. But the values that underlie and frame the democratic spectrum, as expressed in the core ideals of hierarchy and equality, market and mixed society, fission and fusion, simplicity and complexity, do not erode as quickly.[5]

It has long been claimed by conservatives that television is biased in the opposite direction. Responses to that critique, particularly from within the television industry, have typically asserted that television is neither liberal nor conservative, and has no intrinsic political agenda, but is simply commercially driven. Academic critiques of television run the gamut (although here left field is more crowded than right) without agreeing on a single cause or effect of its power. I will suggest that there are grains of truth in all of these points of view, while urging an interpretation that none would likely accept. It is generally true, for example, that the sociology of television production (both journalistic and entertainment) offers a profile that is more liberal than those of many other professions. It is likewise true that on certain important occasions television has mobilized liberal constituencies; but that does not make television an agent of liberalism. And most American TV programming is indeed shaped around commercial interests; but that does not make television an exclusively philistine, commercial, or politically neutral institution.

The argument of *The Sound Bite Society* is framed, in different ways, as a challenge to all points on the ideological spectrum — as well as to the misguided view that the spectrum itself is defunct. But I am loath to call it "bipartisan" — a much abused term, often used to impart an aroma of neutrality to what is merely a dim indifference or hostility to principled commitment. Despite certain ideological trimmings for which I make no apologies, the broader argument should be of interest to conservatives, whose ascendancy it seeks to explain in an era of rising inequality, middle-class insecurity, and globalization, and amid the increasing complexity of technology, society, and everyday life. The lessons, if any, are for liberals, for whom it paints a bleaker picture: the greater challenge they face in battling the electronic currents of a sound bite society.

Although an unabashed "complexitarian," my primary aim is not to advocate complexity. Like simplicity, complexity has its limits in politics and in the life of the mind: obscurantism, scholasticism, elitism. (Marxism is undoubtedly the most complex and original social theory ever advanced, but also the most difficult and obscure — and, lacking any explicit political blueprint, the one most perverted by posterity.) But these deficiencies are not intrinsic to the complexitarian world view. Likewise, simplicity is a natural ally of inequality and exclusion — but not a necessary partner of vulgarity, bigotry, or chauvinism.

The Sound Bite Society is neither a work of philosophy nor one of social science or journalism; to call it an "essay" is to acknowledge a multitude of sins. The argument aims to intrigue and provoke, not to settle any matters with finality. The vast universe of television can be viewed through many lenses—including those of the social sciences, technology, history, religion, communication and film theory, and media criticism. We will focus on the underlying divisions that define us as democratic citizens, and how television functions as a prism for those differences: how it mediates knowledge and values, and the implications of that mediation.

This is accomplished in several stages. We begin in chapter one by looking at the rise of the "Electronic Right," and challenging the familiar claim that the media are liberal. Chapter two analyzes the distinctive communicative language of television and its simplifying tendencies; chapter three considers the forms of simplification—even inherently complex forms—implicit in TV's overall picture of reality. In chapter four, we examine the concept of complexity itself and its political implications. Finally, chapter five explores how the rhetoric of the "Electronic Right" simplifies and distorts discourse, and how the left might respond.

4 · *Some Preliminary Definitions*

Before proceeding, it might help to have clearer working definitions of 'liberalism' and 'conservatism.' Let me briefly suggest a preliminary model of the continuum these words usefully describe:

1 · The terms 'liberal' and 'conservative' (or 'left' and 'right') are relative ones, implying a spectrum of belief between general poles. One could add 'socialist' to identify the farther left end of the democratic spectrum, however marginal in American politics; but in general parlance, 'liberal' and 'conservative' are conceived more or less as opposing bands on a shared spectrum.

2 · On any definition, liberalism is more egalitarian and con-

servatism less so; this is the defining difference between the poles of the spectrum. As "small-d" democrats, liberals and conservatives alike subscribe to the ideal of legal and political equality, as commonly understood in terms of the basic rights of citizenship. They differ, chiefly, about economic equality.

3 · Along with (or implicit within) the basic political equalities, liberals and mainstream conservatives agree in according a certain moral equality to all citizens: equality of dignity or respect, which translates as civic tolerance of harmless differences (leaving aside what constitutes 'harm'). On the extreme right, such equal dignity is denied, reflecting various forms and degrees of intolerance and bigotry. In short: while all democratic ideologies subscribe to a baseline of political equality, *all* forms of conservatism are less egalitarian than rival liberal arguments, and the more extreme forms are also less tolerant.

4 · Underlying these differences over equality, as I will argue later, are different levels of social, moral, and intellectual complexity. A medium that thrives on simple messages, and punishes complex ones, is therefore (for better or worse) more hospitable to conservatism than to liberalism.

Obviously there is more than one kind of liberal or conservative, and no definitions of these charged terms can be definitive or unexceptionable; the framework offered here is a model of the political spectrum, not a precise map or mirror of all shades of political belief. It identifies general values, not positions on particular issues, or the varieties of texture, nuance, idiosyncrasy, contradiction, hypocrisy, or pathology that may characterize particular viewpoints. As such, this model in no way vitiates other descriptive or analytical approaches, such as those that distinguish between social conservatives, who are lower on the tolerance scale, and business conservatives or libertarians, who are more tolerant but not economic egalitarians, etc.[6] History, religion, ethnicity, heredity, life experience—any of these factors may influence a person's belief structure. I am more concerned here with the conceptual and normative core of those beliefs.

5 · *The Complexity Paradox*

Two related ideas, among others, informed and inspired this project. One is the increasing plausibility to me (along with critics on the left) of viewing electronic media in a wider cultural context, as systematic simplifiers of politics and culture in general. This does not imply a conscious conspiracy to simplify—every social pattern or systemic phenomenon need not be of concerted human design—but rather that such simplification occurs anyway, willy-nilly, and occurs generically within the media. As pervasive as it is, television is an inherently partial, selective, and tinted mirror of society; to a great extent it cannot be otherwise. To understand it fully is to examine concealed meanings, structures, and effects, and to make otherwise obscured or neglected distinctions and connections. And to examine in this way, I will suggest, is (depending how far one goes) an essentially liberal or radical enterprise.

The second idea is that whether, or how far, one accepts the first proposition—and consequently, how closely one examines, how much one reveals, how far one distinguishes and connects—in effect, how complex a world one chooses to see—is a quintessentially ideological decision. It is not based on reasoned judgement but on ingrained habits of mind; and such proclivities can be usefully understood as oppositional ones, tending toward either a simpler or a more complex understanding—not

just of television, but of morality, politics, and society in general.
Here, I will suggest, are the very wellsprings of political belief.
One can be deeply committed to a particular political viewpoint
(in terms of the first proposition) and yet, because of the second,
remain agnostic as to the ultimate superiority of radical, liberal,
or conservative ideology.

I have not followed the path of those who view ideology in an
extremely broad context, as a normative framework in which
popular media comprise a single, vast web of belief or propaganda. But neither do I claim that these theorists have it entirely
wrong, or that values do not metastasize into every fiber and seam
of the social fabric. My approach is that of an obstinate if (in the
aforementioned sense) agnostic liberal, saddled with a conservative temperament and radical sympathies. But we might note
in passing a paradoxical feature of the more radical world view—
the view, that is, of those who are linked to the democratic left
by a commitment to equality; by intellectual foundations of a
more integrated, systemic, and complex character; and by a common tradition rooted in Enlightenment liberalism, democratic
socialism, Marxism, critical theory, and related appeals to human
liberation from institutional power structures.

The paradox is this: on one hand, the radical perspective is
more democratic and inclusive than traditional conservatism or
even (on most views) liberalism. Indeed, at its best it aspires to be
ideally democratic and inclusive: the ultimate agent of human liberation. But the very intricacy of radical thought, in the theoretical architecture it employs to expose the cultural and economic
hierarchies of capitalist society, is exclusionary in a different sense.
It is a mind-set committed to seeing more broadly and deeply—
but one which thereby isolates radical thinkers from others and

from the dominant (or "hegemonic") views of mainstream society. Leftist critiques of the media are not just more egalitarian and holistic, but also more penetrating and complex, at times to the point of obscurity. At the extreme, they can be implausibly conspiratorial, depicting capitalism as a concerted and monolithic system of oppression. As such, their terms of debate are—almost necessarily —exclusionary.[7]

Thus, radicals are lonely prophets, decrying conditions and effects that the rest of society fails or declines to recognize. They are forever pulling back the curtain of social reality to unmask hidden complexities that others cannot or will not see. And doing so invites a different kind of hierarchy, and a different elite, of prophets of complexity. (Much of the rhetoric of the left in fact contains a kind of embedded complexity: terms, ideas, and assumptions—including domination, relations of production, cultural hegemony, construction of reality, consciousness, framing, and radical uses of the term 'ideology'—that never surface on television, and even in print serve as markers for complicated concepts with long histories of their own.) This may explain why radical theories are securely ensconced within the walls of academe, and perennially compelling to sophisticated scholars, but have little traction within the institutions of those whom they aspire to liberate—such as labor unions, civil rights organizations, and more nebulous populist movements.

6 · *The Medium in the Mirror*

A few final caveats are in order. There are certain irreducible differences—as well as obvious connections—between print, radio, and audiovisual media, which complicate the exercise of writing about TV, or about one medium and not others. The unique bundle of transmission capabilities that identify a particular medium is by definition irreproducible in another. Thus, it is somewhat artificial—but practically necessary—to isolate television from, e.g., radio, film, or the emerging terrain of cyberspace. Accordingly, this book will focus on television more or less exclusively.[8] It will also look at TV more or less generically, irrespective of content or genre: at its unifying structure and characteristics as a filter of ideas and values.

But what distinguishes television most of all as a shaper of popular consciousness and behavior is its sheer ubiquity and pervasiveness: most of us watch TV far more than we watch films, listen to radio, or read. The universe it mirrors for us is vast, and that mirroring process is the cultural equivalent of breathing. While the medium's impact on political thinking might presumably be especially evident in TV news, and perhaps most of all in political advertising, I have not found it useful to confine my focus to any of these genres or to stress their boundaries over their common features. George Gerbner, the dean of American television scholars, made the point (if perhaps too strongly) two decades ago:

> All types of programming . . . complement and reinforce one another. It makes no sense to study the content or impact of one type of program in isolation from the others. The same viewers watch them all; the total system as a whole is absorbed into the mainstream of common consciousness.[9]

As limited and distortive as its lens can be, television reflects an astonishing range of mediated experience to a huge audience. Thus, to note its limitations is not to suggest that TV is categorically inferior to the written word. As a generator of mediated images, video is manifestly superior to print in certain respects and functions and inferior in others. Moreover, as critics on the right tirelessly point out, much of what appears on TV is intended primarily to entertain, and often succeeds. Even information snobs must concede that this is not entirely a bad thing. "The common man," as one writer has aptly put it, "has a right to be common."[10] Thus, in disparaging TV viewing we must limit our moral condescension. By and large, the harm that results (for adults) is to oneself, not to others; at best it is imprudent, not immoral. While Socratic conversation might be more illuminating for those so inclined, and the telephone may be a better vehicle for malicious gossip, no medium is an exclusive tool of insight or ignorance. But that doesn't mean it is wrong to criticize television's extravagant mediocrity, or that we are a nation of well-informed, critical thinkers and viewers, or that TV serves us well (much less equally well) as citizens.

The extraordinary range of TV's mediating eye, and the size of its audience, may help to explain why its exact effects (if indeed it has "exact" effects) remain elusive even to television scholars. But measuring such effects, even with more rigorous tools than are now at hand, is by no means the only valid form of inquiry. Innumerable books and articles have examined empirical aspects of television; this one will follow a more speculative and analytical route.

After decades of research and argument (and despite ample evidence that television encourages aggression) the nature of TV viewing and its general effects on individual thought and behavior (including on political thought) remain elusive, ambiguous, and controversial. As G.R. Funkhouser and E.F. Shaw note,[11]

... empirical evidence on how manipulations of depicted processes affect audiences is still scarce. Indeed, this research area poses some daunting methodological challenges: specifying, defining, and operationalizing both independent and dependent variables, and separating effects attributable to media causes from a host of plausible confounding variables.

As television scholars routinely note, it is all but impossible to find an adequate "control" group of nonviewers in order to test any hypothesis about the effects of TV viewing.[12] The causal effects of television on political attitudes and political expression are similarly elusive. Gerbner's research in the 1970s and early 1980s (contested by Paul Hirsch in a running dispute in the journal *Communication Research*) has generally suggested a correlation between the amount of viewing and self-identification as a political moderate. But as Gerbner noted in 1987,[13]

> Although heavy viewers tend to prefer the 'moderate' label to both 'conservative' and 'liberal,' the positions they take are closer to that of the conservatives. The most striking political difference between light and heavy viewers in most groups is the collapse of the liberal position as the one most likely to diverge from and challenge traditional assumptions.

Even if heavy viewers are more likely to call themselves moderates, this does not mean television turns otherwise liberal and conservative viewers into moderates, or that TV's effects correlate exclusively with the amount one watches.[14] Nor does it take account of differences between self-designation and actual political performance (voting or advocacy) or the extent to which the political center has drifted to the right in recent decades.

At the same time, it is unlikely that the political and other valences of so diverse a medium flow in a single direction. The influence on thought and behavior of MTV is not necessarily the same as that of the evening news, nature shows, or home shopping. And as psychologists warn, TV is processed differently in the mind of every viewer; no viewer is a purely passive tablet on which media imprint their messages and have their effects. Television, then, undoubtedly has some left- as well as right-tending, and democratic as well as undemocratic, effects.

One thing seems indisputable: while programming has evolved in important ways, the amount and essential nature of viewing hasn't changed radically in a half-century. In this sense, if TV mirrors its immediate times, it is also a more timeless mirror. Some of the most penetrating critiques of the medium (such as by Jerry Mander and Marie Winn) appeared in the 1970s, and the force of their arguments has not dissipated in the intervening years; nor has the force of the more thoughtful "anti-anti-television" counterarguments.[15]

What we do know, particularly from studies of television's connection to aggression and violence, has led to no significant changes in viewing habits or federal regulation. Nor has the political economy of American television essentially changed; its corporate structure and lax regulatory environment had been in place for decades when Jeff Greenfield wrote in 1978 that "What makes television so frightening is that it performs all the functions that used to be scattered among different sources of information and entertainment, and it performs [them] under the control of an almost total monopoly."[16] Since then, despite the expansion of channels via cable and satellite, television's corporate environment has only become more concentrated and less regulated. In essence, out of a well-founded but exaggerated fear of state control of information, we have delivered over control of our mass media—and virtually all popular and political culture—to large corporations that are far less accountable to ordinary citizens than the government we so deeply suspect.

However purportedly neutral or "merely commercial" television is, however beguiling or benumbing, and whatever its measurable effects, *The Sound Bite Society* will show how this master medium, in its very structure, rewards conservatism and punishes liberalism. In making that case, it provides an entirely new rubric for understanding television and politics: the rubric of complexity.

The good news for the right is that, whatever the vagaries of programming or personalities or regulation, television itself, as a simplifying filter, is a handmaiden of conservatism—in both its dignified and more vulgar forms. The good news for the left is that, despite the claims of conservatives eager to serve as its pall bearers, the future of liberalism is not in doubt, in fact it is bright, and suggestions to the contrary misunderstand the very nature of ideological contestation. The left may be moribund or depressed, but these are transient states of play; its more ambitious project—a society based on inclusion, opportunity, security, and tolerance—cannot be annulled or rendered defunct. The obstacles posed by television are serious but not fatal; there remains what Irving Howe called a "margin of hope" for progressive values—as for enlightened conservatism—despite the electronic roadblocks that confront the left in a sound bite society.

The Ascent of the Electronic Right

> [W]hat distinguishes the New Right from other American reactionary movements and what it shares with the early phase of German fascism, is its incorporation of conservative impulses into a system of representation consisting largely of media techniques and media images.
>
> —Philip Bishop[1]

1 · The Pull of the Center and the Rise of the Right

Since the 1960s, and partly in reaction to the liberalizing legacies of that era, the political culture of the United States has drifted steadily to the right. To be sure, the conservative tide is not a single overpowering current; looking at the overall landscape of American politics, one might conclude that the clearest trend is toward the middle and "de-alignment." This is reflected in the rise of independent voters, and the centrist electoral bulge that gave 19 percent of the vote to Ross Perot in 1992: a frustrated blend of economic conservatism, social moderation, and reformist rhetoric that George Gerbner calls "conservative populism." Nevertheless, the stubborn fact remains: in many ways America has become a more conservative nation. The most volatile electoral bloc may huddle in the center, however defined (and the center itself has drifted to the right), fearing both ideological extremes. But the shrinking electorate has clearly shown a much greater propensity for excursions to the right than to the left.

If the ascendancy of Bill Clinton—only the second Democrat

to win the White House in twenty-eight years, and the first to be re-elected since 1944—signified a slowing of the Reagan Revolution of the 1980s, the 1994 midterm did not, as the centrist "bulge" lurched to the right, giving the GOP control of both houses of Congress;[2] and neither did the partisan impeachment of Clinton in 1998-99. There have been no comparable lurches to the left. In the twelve electoral cycles since Watergate, only once (in 1986, as the Iran-Contra scandal was breaking) have Democrats made significant gains in the Senate. Meanwhile, the moderate Republican presence in Congress has dwindled;[3] and forces of the religious right have wrested complete or significant control of more than half of the state Republican parties, a trend that would have seemed unthinkable twenty years ago.[4]

In fact, since the Civil Rights acts of the mid-1960s, there has not been a single great legislative step to the left in America. Clinton's campaign for health care reform in 1994 failed spectacularly and produced the most conservative Congress in modern history. There has been no landmark environmental legislation since the enactment of the Superfund in 1980. The few events that might be construed as liberal victories (such as the defeat of Robert Bork's nomination to the Supreme Court, the Court's upholding of *Roe v. Wade*, or the passage of the Clean Air Act) have been negative victories, deflecting rollbacks rather than making genuine advances—and Pyrrhic ones at that, engendering fierce conservative backlashes. It took an agenda as extreme as Newt Gingrich's 1994 "Contract for America" to give Democrats the middle ground in 1996; and it took the Torquemada tactics of Kenneth Starr's investigation and the subsequent impeachment proceedings in the House Judiciary Committee to provoke the modest but surprising Democratic gains of 1998. What remains to be explained is how Americans could elect a Congress so far to the right of the mainstream in the first place—and why similar swings to the left are almost unimaginable.

Consider where the fulcrum of political debate now lies. Although America is one of the least-taxed and least-regulated industrial democracies, the Republican Congress in the late-1990s did not debate whether to enact a more progressive income tax, but a more radical departure: a highly regressive flat tax—amid talk on the right of abolishing the Internal Revenue Service. Rather than debating how the Federal Communications Commission might define the public interest in the emerging telecommunications environment, Republicans talked of abolishing the FCC and eliminating public broadcasting.

Meanwhile, the Democratic Party's erstwhile base in the South has steadily eroded since the civil rights movement. Labor unions, at least until recently, have remained moribund as a political force; the proportion of the American private labor force that is unionized is lower now than it was in 1935, before the passage of the Wagner Act. Republicans complain disingenuously about the power of labor in the Democratic Party, and seek to neuter unions politically, while themselves thriving on the far greater largesse of corporations. Democrats are perversely accused of being beholden to "special interests," including non-profit advocacy groups, while their accusers accept far more money from private interests motivated by profit.[5] More generally, public control of the economic environment has been undercut simultaneously by the decline of organized labor and the processes of privatization, deregulation, and globalization; the income gap between the haves and have-nots continues to grow; and the Supreme Court, which a generation ago was divided between moderates and liberals, is now split between moderates and ultraconservatives. The far right is undeniably a major force in American politics; the far left is not.

Finally, the term 'liberal' remains a pejorative one in American discourse, used as an epithet by the right, and (at best) in a mildly derogatory way by the media generally; the term 'conservative' bears no such taint. (If the media are composed of liberals, they are self-hating liberals). Democratic candidates at all levels have been routinely labeled as "liberals" by their Republican opponents, on the safe assumption that the word is self-evidently one of opprobrium. Similarly, liberals are equated with a "tax and spend" philosophy, as if taxing and spending were obviously inappropriate functions of government.

It is not impossible to envision a time when the tables will turn: when 'liberal' is no longer anathematic, and politicians on the right cower from the "C-word," hastening to identify themselves as moderates, libertarians, or traditionalists to stress their centrist credentials (as some Republican candidates in less conservative districts were forced to do in 1996, to avoid the extremist taint of Newt Gingrich). But as we enter the twenty-first century, the American agenda is not controlled by the assorted blocs, advocacy groups, unions, nonprofit organizations, and journals of opinion that are the chief agents of liberalism; and the electronic media have hardly been such an agent.

Of course, not all of the messages or effects of television are conservative; it is at least a curiosity that the most rebellious and original generation in American history was also the first to grow up, in the 1950s and 60s, on a steady diet of TV. Moreover, in many of the momentous historical events of that era—McCarthyism, civil rights, Vietnam, Watergate—television played a catalytic role in defeating a conservative cause.[6] But TV has never been an effective tool for addressing the more systemic concerns of the left, such as poverty, progressive taxation, workers' rights, health care, education, children, the elderly, or (except in the dramatic confrontations over segregation) minorities. Conservatives in the television age may have lost some decisive battles, but they have won most of the wars.

2 · *Sound Bite Politics*

It is a truism of our media-dominated age that television has largely usurped the traditional role of the political parties. Power flows to those who control (or can afford to buy access to) the airwaves. The gatekeepers are the arbiters of visibility, such as Ted Koppel and Larry King, and their corporate media masters[7]; party bosses have been replaced by pollsters, media advisers, and direct-mail consultants. Virtually all political actions and communications—not just political ads but also floor speeches by legislators, news conferences, debates, and party conventions— are designed expressly for consumption as sound bites by a TV audience. Television has granted politicians a conduit for reaching audiences with little or no mediation by journalists; but that hardly means it is a neutral conduit, without imperatives and biases of its own.

On its face, this revolution in the nature of political power— the TV Revolution—is old news. It was signalled by the election of John F. Kennedy in 1960, and even earlier, by the TV ad campaign of Dwight D. Eisenhower in 1952. Its roots, like those of TV itself, go back to radio, and Franklin Roosevelt's fireside chats. Yet even as we enter the era of the Internet, we are only beginning to grasp television's unique political role. For some perspective,

we might briefly consider what has happened to our political culture since the historic Kennedy-Nixon debates of 1960 inaugu-
rated television politics as we know it. Recalling those civil,
issue-oriented confrontations, a comment in *The New Yorker*
magazine noted "the almost unbelievable debasement of American political discourse in the intervening thirty years"[8]:

> [N]either man questions the other's integrity or patriotism, suggests
> that a debate between conservative and liberal points of view isn't
> healthy for the country, produces a programmed 'zinger,' resorts
> to a cheap line, delivers a canned speech, or pretends that running
> a government doesn't mean making difficult choices among com-
> peting interests.

Political discourse has indeed been severely coarsened since then;
unquestionably the main reason has been television. And by all
evidence, the winners in the new game of electronic politics have
been on the right, not the left. A Kennedy or a Clinton might
exploit the medium, but as a prism for personal charisma, not as
a conduit of liberal ideas. So might a Martin Luther King, with
his plangent calls for racial justice against a telegenic backdrop
of violent oppression. Yet King's urgent message contained in its
political subtext complex egalitarian goals. Similarly, Sen. Joseph
McCarthy was ultimately undone by television not because of his
conservatism or anticommunism, but because TV allowed the
character traits and tactics of a classic demagogue to overwhelm
ideology. If Kennedy was the first politician to master the medium,
Reagan, North, Gingrich, and Limbaugh—with their simple
right-wing sound bites—are virtually products of it.

The old parties haven't entirely vanished, of course; but
Republicans have adapted to the new realities far more success-

fully than Democrats. GOP-TV, the television arm of the Republican Party, debuted in 1995 with the news magazine *Rising Tide*, a pseudo-news program (less "infotainment" than "infoganda") spreading the conservative gospel and raising money on some two thousand cable systems. At the 1996 Republican National Convention in San Diego, GOP-TV produced a show replete with "anchors" and "reporters," designed to look like a genuine newscast. It was pure propaganda, inspired by the technical and creative wizardry of Ronald Reagan's image-managers, but taken a step further: instead of using timing, locations, and symbols (such as the flag) to influence media coverage, they simply provided the coverage themselves. What they portrayed was a party of tolerance and inclusion, offering genuine hope and opportunity to women, minorities, the disabled, the afflicted: in short, a fairy tale.

The Conservative Television Network (CTN) debuted in 1996, drawing on a data bank of 110 million conservative contributors. Other conservative TV initiatives have included National Empowerment Television (later renamed America's Voice), a twenty-four-hour, C-Span-type network with a right-wing tilt on both cable and satellite, largely sponsored by Paul Weyrich's Free Congress Foundation; and Lamar Alexander's Republican Exchange Satellite Network, sending monthly broadcasts to cable systems nationwide. And in taking to the airwaves, Republicans have merely staked a political claim where right-wing televangelists have mined a mother lode, with messages that overlap and complement those of Republican conservatism. The vast potential audience for such telecasts is a conservative telemarketer's dream: some four million American households, nearly all in rural and suburban areas, that own satellite dishes.

The Democrats have belatedly entered the fray; but as in the use of direct mail, Republicans have been far savvier (and better funded) in using satellite and cable TV, fax networks, and the Internet to spread their messages and mobilize their constituencies. GOP-TV's "slickly packed shows," in the words of Howard Kurtz, "make the Democrats look like they are communicating with tin cans and string."[9] For the left in general, however, technical know-how, and even the lack of support from wealthy foundations, aren't the only barriers to successful competition with the right on the airwaves. In myriad other ways television functions as a brake on liberal messages and values.

3 · *A Thought Experiment*

Before examining those right-tending factors in greater detail, let's consider the following thought experiment. Suppose that it's 1945, a historical turning point in mass communication (as well as in world history), and a nadir of the American right; and you, as a conservative, are free to choose an ideal vehicle, a "dream medium," to purvey your ideas. What would you want that medium to look like?

First, it should appeal to people of all ages, groups, and backgrounds, virtually indiscriminately. More than that, you would want it to be so powerful a force in daily life as to effectively homogenize society, blunting or ignoring the extremes (including those on the far-right whose intolerance discredits your cause). As an orthodox free-market capitalist, you would want the medium to be dominated by large corporate enterprises, not by individuals, government, or groups guided by motives other than profit. You wouldn't want it to gravitate toward issues of narrow concern to working people or minorities, or to points of view that raise the invidious question of class. Instead, you would want it to broadcast, like a fluffy blanket over American consciousness, the comforting notion that we are a great middle-class nation in which people get pretty much what they deserve and no one should complain: the realization of the American Dream. (The ironic thought might occur to you that this is the liberals' ideal. But you take comfort in knowing that their standards for achieving it are utopian; maybe the medium's blanket will fool people into believing that Dream has been achieved.)

The more commercially driven the medium, the better for your cause, because it will focus on the needs, tastes, and interests of affluent and middle-class consumers. Better still if the medium is so potent a commercial force that even the "news" is a commodity driven mainly by entertainment values to maximize its audience, with little time or concern for the investigative journalism and deeper analysis of complex issues that liberals get so worked up about. The medium should ignore or ridicule as "elitist" ideas that are unduly unusual, experimental, egalitarian, or noncommercial; no rocking the boat. The less people think about their connections to others, and society in general, and the more they simply look out for their own material interests, the better for your cause.

If you were truly visionary, your ideal medium would also be a potential vehicle for fundamentalist preaching and fundraising, because given the right communication platform, Christian fundamentalism might prove to be a potent mobilizing force in years hence, in a conservative golden age. Further befitting your inclinations, this medium's news-delivery establishment should be cynical about government and social change; and its news departments should be responsive to the commercial interests of their owners and sponsors, not to some broader public interest, because a commercial medium is after all a business, not a public charity, and why should it bite the hand that feeds it—especially if it's a conservative hand? Even better if the political culture of the medium is such that news reporters are terrified of being branded as "liberals." Political debates on it, if any, should be between two poles: the center and the right.

Finally, but perhaps most important, the native "language" of the medium should be highly adaptable to conservative ideas. It should be driven—economically and technologically—by dramatic, visceral emotional messages that please or anger or incite, not by complex ideas that might make people think or act cooperatively. Send me a medium, you might say, that shuns complicated abstractions while exalting America as a heroic nation standing tall in the world, and the heroic individual—the cowboy, lawman, doctor, warrior, spy, athlete, or private eye. Mr. Sandman, send me a Machine of Simple American Dreams. Now wake up, Mr. and Ms. Conservative, and turn on your TV set.

A closer look at several interrelated features of TV viewing—relating to its content, the nature of viewership, and its economic and institutional environment—will further suggest that it is hardly a reliable agent of liberalism. And that's just part of the story. Television's structure is the rest.

1 · *Immediacy and Superficiality*: By weighting political discourse toward symbols, images, slogans, and sound bites, TV rewards simpler messages. It forces politicians and journalists alike to be more exposure- and image-conscious, focusing their attention (and that of viewing audiences) on the cosmetic and superficial values of individual presentation and away from issues and ideas. More than ever before, politicians must sell themselves, not their ideas. Left and right alike, they have become a soul-less class

of cardboard public figures. These and related structural pressures—to be explored in due course—disproportionately challenge politicians with ideas that are inherently more complex.

2 · *Institutional Amnesia*: Television is in one sense quintessentially "historical": it records the passage of human events in time and space. But (notwithstanding the History Channel) what it mainly offers is a history of the present moment, not a way of understanding or generalizing about the past, present, or future. As a creature of the present, television is often weak or unreliable in conjuring the historical past, and weaker still in conjuring an idealized future. For these and other reasons, it reinforces the status quo, for which conservatives can be thankful.

3 · *Passivity and Narcissism*: Television further challenges core liberal values—equality, tolerance, and the critical spirit—on the microcosmic level of the individual viewer. Though undoubtedly germane, we won't explore the psychological dimension of television viewing except to make a few passing observations.[10] As has been widely observed, TV promotes narcissism and regression in the viewer: mental states that are inimical to the complex, critical, and other-directed modes of thought that are the foundations of liberalism. It is often argued that the narcotizing passivity and mindless consumption engendered by endless hours of viewing are inherently reactionary states of awareness or inactivity. At the very least, it's hard to see how such passivity would lend itself to a spirit of activism, egalitarianism, or a zeal for change.[11] Television literally diminishes the world for us, scaling it down to fit on the screen. Far more than it unites, television "isolates people from the environment, from each other, and from their own senses."[12]

With its invitation to voyeurism, TV evokes a kind of empathy for humanity's weak or abnormal that is wholly passive and risk-free. At the same time, it affords us a false sense of power and control and of the world's manageability. "Larger than the figures on the screen," writes Robert Stam, "we quite literally oversee the world from a sheltered position—all the human shapes parading before us in television's insubstantial pageant are scaled down to lilliputian insignificance, two-dimensional dolls whose height rarely exceeds a foot." In the process, "we see without being seen and hear without being heard."[13] In addition to these structural features, commercial TV programming, including news, is expressly designed not to offend. "In psychoanalytic terms," writes Stam, "television promotes a narcissistic relationship with an imaginary other. It infantilizes in the sense that the young child perceives everything in relation to itself; everything is ordered to the measure of its ego."

4 · *Conformity and Homogeneity*: In terms of the messages conveyed by its content, TV is a powerful vehicle of homogeneity and mass conformity; in George Comstock's words, it "smooths the social hierarchy without disrupting it." Historically, TV's reflection of society has been bland and uniform, denying the social, ethnic, economic, religious, and political diversity of American culture. In the 1950s, writes Todd Gitlin,[14] ". . . the television networks were crucial dispensers of America's master idea of itself. . . .

> Television was a school for manners, mores, and styles; for repertories of speech and feeling; even for personality. Television helped teach Americans how to talk, look, and behave—which meant, in some measure, teaching them how they should think, how they should feel, and how, perchance, they should dream.

Despite recent trends toward greater diversity, TV still celebrates the "normal" nuclear middle-class white family that it worshipped in the 1950s, and that also happens to be its primary advertising niche market. It still perpetuates stereotypes, although less monolithically than before, and creates and encourages "norms" of white middle-class America with which commercial sponsors are comfortable. The poor, the homeless, and other out-groups seldom find the TV camera's eye, except on the news when engaged in violent acts. Overall, it would be hard to conclude that television has promoted diversity, individuality, or innovative or unpopular thought or behavior.

Television programming, in fact, has reinforced traditional conservative frameworks in many ways: the stereotyping of gender roles, particularly on children's programs; the relatively scant and distorted portrayals of minorities,[15] the poor, the elderly, the disabled, working people, activists and politically committed people, and (pace Ellen DeGeneres) lesbians and homosexuals; the narcissism and hedonism of many characters, and the emphases on wealth, power, and sex as preeminent human values. Through this homogenizing process, television blurs the perception of (but does not alter) social and class boundaries. It is a great leveller of taste, experience, and ideas, and of class awareness, but not of class itself. In a sense (however illusory or false), we all partake of the synthetic middle-class existence that television projects.[16]

When not defining and validating the cultural mainstream, TV is awkward and inauthentic. It is hard, for instance, to recall a single compelling portrayal of the 1960s counterculture — one of the most significant cultural and generational schisms in American history. TV's depictions of that counterculture — as (at least until recently) of gays, feminists, spiritualists, and political activists — have been few and largely stereotypical. (A corollary of this "mainstreaming effect" is that TV characters, for example in soap operas and sitcoms, often have no cultural context, and no real spiritual, political, or intellectual lives.)

Ironically, while television exalts American individualism, it is distinctly biased against genuine originality. It doesn't lavish attention on the solitary voices of iconoclasts, dissidents, pathfinders, loners, or misfits. TV's oddballs, from Maynard G. Krebs and Gilligan to Felix Unger and Cosmo Kramer, are figures of fun, never people to be taken seriously. TV promotes individualism not as social independence, but in heroic terms, and in terms of physical isolation and moral and political detachment. Among viewers, it rewards isolation and discourages involvement, enabling us, to a unique extent, to experience the world vicariously—and in ways far exceeding the scope of daily life—while remaining alone, passive, and even in bed.

5 · *The Existential Self:* The prevailing political ethos of Hollywood is indeed a liberal one, and this is sometimes reflected on television—for example, in a general social tolerance, and skepticism toward large corporations. But TV's messages are more often populist than liberal in the stronger sense. They are seldom genuinely egalitarian, pro-labor, or pro-government; they reinforce, rather than break down, social, gender, racial, and class stereotypes.[17] Underdogs are rarely highlighted; law-enforcement programs do not advance public awareness of civil liberties, police brutality, or flaws in the criminal justice system. Nor does TV often depict the less visible or telegenic social contributions of those lower on the social scale, such as factory workers, teachers, writers, musicians, artists, or social workers.

The stress on heroic middle-class professionals, and the corresponding inability to depict larger groups, movements, or institutions, reinforces an existential framework in which individuals, not systems or collectivities, are the locus of power and both the cause and the solution to social problems. And this is a pillar of the simpler, more conservative model of society. Even when portraying economic exploitation or discrimination in ways that jibe with liberal themes, or characters who are poor, female, minorities, etc., TV is inept at showing the more complex, long-term, and institutional remedies that characterize liberalism.

An especially pervasive theme of TV programming is the glorification of law-enforcement personnel. While some of the cop shows are excellent, most of them (and much of local news) distort public perceptions of crime and violence and contribute to a siege mentality among viewers. As many studies have shown, heavier viewers are more prone to exaggerate the actual incidence of violent crime, an effect that George Gerbner and other television scholars call the "Mean World" syndrome. TV imparts a perception that the world is more dangerous than it actually is— what James Fallows calls "a fatalistic, protect-what-I've-got mentality" in which "every TV market can get the impression that life has turned into a *Blade Runner*ish hell"[18]—a view that encourages simple, forceful measures to protect society from those dangers.

Several corollaries of these various conservatizing tendencies of television seem especially relevant here. One is the marginalization of dissenting and nonconformist practices and beliefs, which (except for extreme-right militants) are disproportionately found on the left. In this respect, TV arguably has a dampening effect on social tolerance. Another is the further marginalizing of already marginal ethnic and social minorities. A third corollary is that TV delegitimizes social class as an issue (in fact it is virtually taboo), without altering class structure. And class structure is something liberals, not conservatives, want to talk about.

4 · Economic and Regulatory Barriers

One of the most obvious ways in which television functions as a conservative force in American society relates to the obvious fact that it is a preeminently commercial medium, dominated by large corporations whose primary interest is the bottom line. That interest is antithetical to the liberal agenda, which is archetypically concerned with noncommercial goods and values and off-market modes of distribution. "Television," as one writer succinctly puts it, "is fundamentally a marketing device. Its values are the values of the marketplace; its structure and content mirror that purpose."[19] TV advertising is the electronic linchpin of consumer capitalism: a relentless invitation to self-indulgence, acquisitiveness, and unlimited consumption.

TV fiction supports these ends not just in its dependence on commercial advertising but also in its content, which tends to celebrate affluence and acquisitiveness as normal, while ignoring activities such as voluntarism, community activism, political engagement, or other pursuits or careers that involve self-sacrifice or personal connections to larger groups or causes. In addition to further marginalizing the already marginal, commercial TV projects a world dominated by greed, banality, guile, lust, and violence.[20] It shuns the experimental, the unusual, and the controversial in favor of what is safe, conventional, and traditional—a formula hardly conducive to radical (or even democratic) ideas. Indeed, the "formula" central to commercial television's profitability is formularism itself—hence the plethora of reruns, spin-offs, and sequels, and the lackluster, derivative nature of most (though certainly not all) programming since the "Golden Age" of the 1950s. It is hardly a model of human nature and society that liberals would choose to promote.

Public television, intended as an alternative to such commercialism, has failed in its mission as envisioned by the Carnegie Commission in 1967: to provide a noncommercial venue for excellence, diversity, and independent voices. Its convoluted bureaucracy has been dominated by (often conservative) political appointees with no interest in excellence or controversy. Pockets of excellence have survived, as tools of corporate identification for Mobil Oil, Archer Daniels Midland, and other industrial giants. But the independent documentaries that are part of the cream of American journalism have been largely shut out of the system, which remains beholden to Congress and corporate underwriters. And under pressure from the right, the congressional appropriation for public broadcasting was slashed to a pitiful $250 million in 1998—a tiny fraction of what other nations spend per citizen.[21]

Meanwhile, the increasing concentration of the commercial media, with a dozen or so giant conglomerates—Disney, Time-Warner, General Electric, Westinghouse, Viacom, Rupert Murdoch's News Corporation, et al.—controlling the main stream of information to American households, is hardly a recipe for liberal reform. This trend, amply documented elsewhere, nonetheless warrants mention here. Robert W. McChesney sums it up: "The preponderance of US mass communication is controlled by less than two dozen enormous profit-maximizing corporations, which receive much of their income from advertising placed largely by other huge corporations."[22] Lack of diversity, self-censorship, and other troubling conflicts and compromises between news values and commercial interests are just some of the ways in which media conglomerates disserve the public interest by putting profit first.

An even more tangible economic barrier to the left is the fact that, in a political world driven by costly TV spots, candidates and causes of the right have more access to individual and corporate wealth. Although his immediate competitors were fellow Republicans, Ronald Reagan said more than he knew when he quipped during a debate before the 1980 New Hampshire primary: "I paid for this microphone." By vastly increasing the power of money, television raises the ante of political finance, which in turn favors conservative candidates. Business PACs, for instance, far outspend those of organized labor.

More generally, what I am calling the Electronic Right comprises a broad alliance of elected officials, journalists, broadcasters, and intellectuals, whose access to the media is supported by deep conservative reservoirs such as the Sarah Scaife and Carthage foundations (both controlled by Richard Mellon Scaife), and the Olin, Smith-Richardson, J.M., and Bradley foundations. This policy-marketing machine sponsors an assortment of leading think tanks (such as the Heritage Foundation, American Enterprise Institute, Cato Institute, Hudson Institute, Manhattan Institute, and the Hoover Institution); various newspapers, magazines, journals, and media pressure groups; conferences and seminars, books and articles, research studies, speaking engagements, editorial briefing sessions, and Internet projects; "astroturf" (fake grassroots) campaigns; radio and TV shows, including the public television programs of William F. Buckley, Peggy Noonan, William Bennett, and Ben Wattenberg, among others; and sundry antitax and antiregulatory organizations.[23] Foundations on the left have vastly inferior resources, which must be allocated across a broader agenda of social service and grassroots activism besides media. As a result, liberals in the 1980s and 90s have scarcely been able to match the conservatives' well-oiled propaganda machine.

Finally, the deregulation of broadcasting, beginning in the Reagan Administration, has not made television a more liberal force, but rather has given broadcasters a freer hand to generate profits free of public-interest regulation. Since passage of the Federal Communications Act of 1934, a condition of license renewal had been that broadcasters operate "in the public convenience, interest and necessity." Now, rules regarding how many TV stations a company can own, and how quickly they can be bought and resold, have been relaxed. The modest balancing mechanism of the Fairness Doctrine was rescinded in 1987; and the public interest standard, as a basis for relicensing stations, has become a national joke; the fox rules the chicken coop. Mark S. Fowler, the first FCC chairman under Reagan who theorized that television is just "a toaster with pictures," deregulated with a vengeance, even lifting rules prohibiting program-length commercials aimed at children. Freed of all meaningful public interest regulations, the broadcast industry boomed. In a monumental twist of the meaning of public interest, Fowler maintained that "the commission will defer to a broadcaster's judgement about how best to compete for viewers and how best to attract and sustain the public's interest."[24]

The 1996 Telecommunications Act made matters even worse—much worse—by further relaxing the license renewal process, deregulating cable rates, and giving station owners the right to acquire additional stations. Broadcasters, in turn, spent more than $3.2 million on soft money contributions to national political organizations in the 1995–96 election cycle. Even more scandalous, however, was the giveaway to broadcasters, without asking for bids and with virtually no public debate, of the new digital frequency spectrum, a public resource with an auction value estimated at up to $70 billion. (The present analog spectrum will be phased out by the year 2006). This gift from tax-payers to media conglomerates, courtesy of the US Congress, even outraged some conservatives; Bob Dole called it "the biggest single gift of public property to any industry in this century." William Safire added, "It's as if each American family is to be taxed $1,000 to enrich the stockholders of Disney, GE and West-inghouse."[25]

5 · *The Quasi-Myth of Liberal Bias in the Media*

Mainstream journalists are widely depicted by the right as a liberal group; and, by and large, they are more liberal in their personal views than the rest of American society, as are many TV and film writers and producers. But there are also institutional, professional, and cultural reasons why those views are not reflected in the news product, and why the national press corps as a whole tends to be more centrist or apolitical than liberal. For these and other reasons, progressive viewpoints have been largely marginalized within the corporate milieu of commercial television.

Journalists are inclined to be more skeptical toward the public sector, which is the focus of much of their coverage, than toward the private sector for which they work; they are often hostile to ideology per se, and (particularly since Watergate) hostile to liberal ideology. "When it comes to the news itself," writes

Everette E. Dennis, ". . . the most popular story for the media in this [or] any decade is that 'Government doesn't work'. . . in story after story, they point up the follies and foibles of government, government officials, and politicians."[26] Government waste, bureaucratic inefficiency, corruption, and pork barrel politics are certainly important journalistic targets. Yet only in the most scandalous cases do journalists report on waste, corruption, or social dislocation caused by the private sector. Television is inept at depicting, and thus reticent about, things that government does well, where the social benefits are often gradual, invisible, or indirect—such as a Head Start program, a college loan, or food and drug regulation. Occasions when government performs with dramatic, visible efficacy—such as space shots, rescues, disaster relief, FBI stings, limited military actions—seldom translate into confidence in the public sector.

Furthermore, professional standards of neutrality and social factors alike encourage among most reporters a political bias toward the middle of the road. Mark Hertsgaard has documented the docility of the media toward Ronald Reagan; "The press," Sam Donaldson told him, "myself included, traditionally sides with authority and the establishment."[27] And this is how Robert Darnton recalls the atmosphere at the *New York Times* in the 1960s:[28]

> You often hear that newsmen tend to be liberals or Democrats, and as voters they may indeed belong to the left. But as reporters, they generally struck me as hostile to ideology, suspicious of abstractions, cynical about principles, sensitive to the concrete and the complex, and therefore apt to understand, if not condone, the status quo. They seemed scornful of preachers and professors and quick with pejoratives like 'do-gooder' and 'egghead.' Until some social psy-

chologist devises a way to make an inventory of their value system, I am inclined to disagree with the common contention that journalism suffers from a liberal or left-wing bias.

As we shall see, inclinations toward particularity, immediacy, and simplicity are defining features of conservatism— and also of daily journalism, especially in electronic media. Journalism as a profession (and television in particular), is not a noted haven for theoreticians, or even for critical or analytic thinkers. Austin Ranney, among other political scientists, argues that for professional reasons journalists tend to be more or less equally biased— to the point of cynicism—against *all* politicians. Summarizing research (by Edward Jay Epstein and others) on journalists' political views, Ranney observes that:[29]

> The overwhelming majority [of journalists] have quite apolitical backgrounds. Almost none have a longstanding relationship with a political cause or organization, and almost none have ever worked for a political party or candidate. Indeed, over two-thirds claim never to have registered to vote as a member of a political party.

Ranney points out that while more journalists identify themselves as liberal than conservative, what they mean by the term 'liberal' tends to equate with a public watchdog role and a vague sense of professional fairmindedness. Worthy as these ideals are, they are dubious tokens of liberalism as an ideology not just of tolerance but of greater economic equality.

6 · *Institutional Barriers: Who's Tilting the Screen?*

Several recent trends further underscore television's increasing power as a vehicle of conservative ideas. These include the political orientation of high-visibility pundits and commentators; the tabloidization of TV news and the flourishing in the past decade of "soft" and tabloid shows, and the concurrent decline and dilution of both local and national network news; and the emergence of televangelism and the religious right. In different ways, each of these trends bears signatures of the conservative agenda and reflects television's amenability to simple, emotive, self-regarding messages, and its corresponding aversion to complexity.

For all their alleged liberal bias, in recent decades the networks and public television have been decidedly more hospitable to the showcasing of centrist and conservative voices. With rare exceptions, guests on public affairs programs are fonts of conventional wisdom, typically powerful Beltway insiders with views running the gamut from right to center. The fulcrum of debate on the talk shows is even further to the right: for every centrist or moderate liberal on the left side of the screen, (e.g., Shields, Germond, Carlson, Clift, Carville, Stephanopoulos), there is a crowd on the right and center-right: Barnes, Bay Buchanan, Pat Buchanan, Buckley, Gergen, Glassman, Kondracke, Krauthammer, Kristol, Limbaugh, McLaughlin, Matalin, Novak, Safire, Snow, Stassinopoulos, Sununu, Wattenberg, Will, et al.

In addition, conservative and centrist think tanks are cited in the mainstream media far more often than those on the left.[30] (For that matter, the nation's opinion pages are likewise tilted to the right;[31] and, contrary to popular belief, "every conservative candidate from Nixon in 1968 to Bush in 1988 received between 60 percent and 80 percent of daily newspaper endorsements"[32].) But as a polemical strategy, the right's allegation of "liberal bias" has succeeded in convincing the post-Watergate media of the untruth that they lean to the left. One can argue ad infinitum about who is a "conservative" and who a "liberal," and obviously there are many ideological shades; but it is clear enough that the left is underrepresented on television, and even misrepresented by more centrist figures. Right-wing fireworks, with their sparks of extremism, bigotry, and invective, are what sell audiences, not moderate or progressive arguments.

The balance is even more lopsided on talk radio, pitched to narrower and more conservative drive-time audiences and dominated by a cadre of tough-talking conservatives and right-wing demagogues: Limbaugh, Don Imus, Bob Grant, G. Gordon Liddy, Michael Reagan, Oliver North, Bay Buchanan, David Duke, Paul Harvey, Barry Farber, Morton Downey, Jr., Neal Boortz, Armstrong Cunningham, and legions of small-market imitators. (The rare liberal exceptions, with fewer stations and smaller audiences, include Jim Hightower, Diane Rehm, and Jerry Brown; others, such as Mario Cuomo, Gary Hart, and Joycelyn Elders, had brief careers as talkers before their shows were canceled.)

Unlike TV, which must attract wider audiences, much of the right-wing radio talk is virulent and bigoted, with visceral sound bites and slurs that might make a Novak or a McLaughlin shudder, and arguments at a level of critical rigor that wouldn't get past editors at the *New York Post*. Callers to the radio talk shows tend to echo the views of their right-wing hosts; dissenters are summarily disconnected, typically with an insult.[33] And the shows are a potent political force. Sen. James Inhofe (R-Oklahoma), one of the most conservative members of the US Senate, told a panel discussion on radio and politics in 1997, "I would not be here except for talk radio."[34]

Rush Limbaugh, who began his syndicated radio program in

1988 and added a TV show in 1992, was the dominant figure on the Electronic Right in the 1990s, with a combined TV and radio audience estimated to run as high as 20 million people. Unlike more dignified conservatives—such as Will, Safire, Thomas Sowell, or Kevin Phillips—Limbaugh doesn't engage in reasoned debate or thoughtful commentary. Instead, he is an extraordinarily efficient invective machine, a font of name-calling, ridicule, ad hominem argument, context removal, and other offenses against critical thinking. Demonizing liberal and media "elites" in the name of populism, he mobilizes the most intolerant and anti-egalitarian segments of the hate-driven far-right. Indeed, it is one of the great ironies of our time that while the left has floundered, the right has marshalled populist sentiments of powerlessness, resentment and alienation, and painted the far more egalitarian politics of liberalism as elitist.

There have always been Limbaughs on the right, beginning with the radio preachers of the 1930s. Why are there no Limbaughs of the center or left, and what accounts for the sudden spread of Limbaugh-style hate radio in the 1990s as a political force? Michael Lerner suggests that it is partly a response to the banality of most political coverage and debate on mainstream television: "Compared to this seemingly neutered and energy-depleted reality, hate radio feels alive and much less phony."[35] E.J. Dionne, Jr.,[36] speculates that there are no prominent Limbaugh counterparts on the center or left because,

> conservatism now enjoys a mass popular appeal that liberalism does not. The mass movements of liberalism, in the labor and civil rights movements, for example, are in decline, while popular

movements on the right, such as the Christian conservatives and the pro-gun movements, are on the upswing. Certainly the managers of local radio stations seem to find that conservative programs are a larger draw than moderate or liberal programs.

Dionne's point is well-taken, but doesn't fully explain the ascent of the Electronic Right and the decline of the left; in a sense, it merely restates the question. There are certainly issues on the left's agenda—health care, job security and safety, education, environmental protection—that appeal to mass audiences. Perhaps a more complete answer is that what we debate in our democracy is partly defined by the tools of debate; that television took several decades to reach its maturity as a political medium; and that the complexity of liberalism makes its messages resistant to popular media. It's not that there aren't vulnerable audiences who are potentially receptive to the messages of the left; but their vulnerabilities center on structural elements in society and corporate excesses, rather than threats to one's class status from below. The simpler and more egocentric tenets of conservatism (while seldom as polemical and factually challenged as Limbaugh's work) are ready-made for radio and television news and shout shows. As Bruce Morton, the veteran CBS News correspondent, observed in 1988: "One of [Dukakis's] problems in this whole campaign has been that his message doesn't 'sound-bite' as easily."[37]

Thus, a political mantra such as "no new taxes" requires little explanation (except, of course, for how to deal with the ensuing deficit when tax cuts fail to generate the added revenues promised by Reaganomics). In contrast, the more egalitarian aims of the left, even when they can be compressed into slogans, are

more pregnant and complex ("Read my lips: some new taxes"?)
and require more explanation than electronic media normally tolerate. Outrage at tax increases plays well on the air; it is a simple,
self-regarding conservative idea. Arguments for equalizing public school finance are less sound-bite-ready.[38]

7 · *Broadcasting and the Religious Right*

Sound bites are not the only answer to the Limbaugh conun-
drum; and however distorted or selective the picture, TV's reflection of American society—unlike that of radio—is at least in
some respects a force for tolerance. Whereas radio can narrow-
cast to smaller audiences, racism, bigotry, anti-Semitism, xeno-
phobia, and contempt for deviant lifestyles rarely find explicit
expression on the tube. There is one major exception to this generality, however: since the 1970s, TV has been an unparalleled
vehicle of Christian fundamentalism, scarcely an agent of tolerance or equality.

Preachers of the gospel have become TV fixtures: from Rev.
Jerry Falwell's *Old-Time Gospel Hour*—a springboard for the
founding of the Moral Majority and the Liberty Lobby—to Pat
Robertson's *700 Club* on his Christian Broadcasting Network, a
precursor of the Family Channel (available in 59 million American homes as of 1996), and many others: Robert H. Schuller's
Hour of Power, with its worldwide audience of more than 20 million; Oral Roberts and Garner Ted Armstrong, Reverend Ike,
Rex Humbard, and the disgraced Jimmy Swaggart and Jim
Bakker. For all their religious content, these shows are also highly
commercial in nature; indeed, in many respects—product development and promotion, brand loyalty, market segmentation, pre-
miums, telethons, the squeezing out of local competition from

neighborhood churches—the telemarketing of fundamentalist religion is a classic commercial enterprise. The electronic ministries have raised, by conservative estimates, hundreds of millions of untaxed dollars annually while offering scripture, prophecy, and faith healing. The Rev. Billy Graham has stood out from the televangelist pack in eschewing overt partisanship, fund-raising, and intolerance of other faiths.

One reason for the effectiveness of televangelism is its promise of redemption. It elicits the confirming act of sending money, ostensibly to pay for the conversion of unbelievers. And it creates between viewers and preacher the same kind of false intimacy, a highly artificial and one-way sense of proximity, as it does between viewers and Hollywood stars or political or sports figures. Needless to say, none of the religious broadcasters is associated with progressive values. Christian fundamentalism focuses the individual inward and toward Christ rather than toward the more tolerant and egalitarian spirit, and the good works and voluntarism that other Christian denominations have brought to American culture. Its main claim on government is for the legal enactment of its own teachings, by demanding, for example, prayer in public schools. With strict adherence to church dogma comes intolerance of divergent beliefs and practices, a sense of moral superiority, and—the essence of any fanaticism—messianic ambitions to convert others to one's own faith. Those teachings are essentially simple and authoritarian, anchored in the fear of God, the power of prayer, the charisma of the preacher, and the literal and infallible truth of the Bible. They offer a single solution to life's problems: accept Christ, and everything else will sort itself out.

The Federal Communications Commission—like the Internal

Revenue Service—has historically taken a very tolerant view of televangelism. In 1965, the FCC declared religious broadcasters to be exempt from the (now defunct) Fairness Doctrine. The National Association of Broadcasters' television code—which forbids the advertisement of such public dangers as occultism, fortune telling, and astrology—calls on stations to apportion religious programming time "fairly among responsible individuals, groups and organizations." But by the time the fundamentalists emerged on TV in the 1970s, the more mainstream, interfaith religious programs that had been a Sunday morning staple of the networks in the 1950s and 60s (such as *Frontiers of Faith* (NBC), *Look Up and Live* (CBS), *Lamp Unto My Feet* (CBS), *Directions* (ABC), *The Catholic Hour*, and the Jewish-oriented *The Eternal Light*) had vanished. Further FCC rulings in the 1960s and 1970s enabled stations to use paid religious broadcasts to satisfy the mandated public service requirement of local stations.[39] The floodgates of right-wing televangelism were open.

With the election of Ronald Reagan in 1980, aided by Falwell's Moral Majority, the powerful marriage of the religious right and television was manifest. An older generation of less political televangelists—Billy Graham, Rex Humbard, Oral Roberts—were now joined on the tube by a new cadre including Falwell, Pat Robertson, Jimmy Swaggart, James Robison, Jim Bakker, et al., with explicit conservative messages and close ties to the New Right through such operatives as Paul Weyrich and Richard Viguerie. As one pair of TV analysts put it, the televangelist programs had become "increasingly political and evaluative, and when evaluative, increasingly univocal."[40] By the mid-1980s, the annual revenues of the religious broadcasters were in excess of a half-billion tax-free dollars.[41] Robertson (CBN), Paul Crouch

(Trinity Broadcasting Network), and Jim Bakker (the PTL Network) had developed satellite-delivered cable broadcast networks, and the total audience for religious programming had grown from some 5 million in the late-1960s to upwards of 25 million.[42]

Falwell's Moral Majority blazed the trail from televangelism to the political arena, branding liberals as atheists and rating officeholders according to how "pro-God" they were. In 1988, Pat Robertson became a force in presidential politics, something no preacher could have done earlier in American history. Although audiences declined after the Bakker and Swaggart scandals, the number of full-time religious stations in metropolitan areas continued to swell. In the 1990s, the Christian Right rebounded as an even more potent political force. Out of the ashes of Falwell's Moral Majority emerged the phoenix of Robertson's Christian Coalition.

8 · *Tabloidization: The News at Twilight*

Since the mid-1980s, TV's antipathy to complexity has been further amplified by two converging trends: the rise of a new breed of tabloid "infotainment" shows that mimic (and at times even outdo) traditional television news, and the concurrent decline of network news, reflected in the defunding of news departments and an increased emphasis on soft, uncontroversial, inexpensive news magazines such as *20/20*, *Dateline NBC*, and *48 Hours*—in short, on commercialism. The emergence of primetime tabloid broadcasting, beginning with Fox Broadcasting's *A Current Affair* (1986) and followed by *Inside Edition* and *Hard Copy* in 1989, is one of the most significant programming developments in the history of the medium, serving up a blend of soft news features, celebrity gossip, scandal, deviance, and lurid crime. At their occasional best, these shows offer serious investigative journalism, along with a refreshing (if spurious) emotional authenticity not found in other mainstream genres.

Television's visual and commercial characteristics are naturally suited to the tabloid style: sensational, heroic, personalized stories with simple narrative structures and conventional underlying values. It is a medium of visual storytelling, not of theorizing: a medium wedded to discrete moments, locations, events, and individuals. The tabloid style, in turn, epitomizes television's bias toward the immediate and superficial, and away from the systemic pattern or condition, the longer trend, the deeper question; it is a journalism of the trivial and of the foreground. The term 'tabloid' is rooted in 'tablet': something condensed or compressed. In American journalism, it came to refer to a short, headline-style format—the nineteenth-century print equivalent of the sound bite—as opposed to the broadsheet.

Despite the superficially apolitical cast of tabloid TV, its style and messages reflect a powerful dispositional bias toward conservatism. In its defiantly trivial world, fame, money, and sex are the resident gods; conflicts are moralistic melodramas between good and evil; nonconformity, dissent, and social problems are abhorrent or invisible. The tabloid shows focus on personalities but not character; celebrity but not moral, intellectual, or artistic distinction; "unsolved mysteries," but not education; lawbreaking and infractions of social rules but not courage or originality. As Graham Knight observes: "Against the greed, corruption, self-interest, and indifference of the powerful, on the one hand, and the moral and physical danger and threat of the deviant, on the other, tabloid sets up the people as the bearers of ordinary virtues. . . ." Tabloid's populism, in Knight's words, "works through a dialectic of security and reassurance on the one hand, and threat and menace on the other."[43]

Tabloid TV is in fact an unconscious parody of television generally: flashy, cynical, assertive, confrontational; demanding instant results, and contemptuous of ambiguity, complexity, originality, creativity, or public enterprise. It exaggerates the very tendencies—to sell, to preach, to shock, to personalize, concretize, and dramatize—that make television structurally conservative. In its signature voice, the clipped, disdainful accent of the middle-brow Australian (perhaps to connote outside authority without seeming dangerously foreign or learned), the tabloid show projects an anarchic world of heroes, villains, and cops: the "Mean World" run riot.

In short, the TV tabs exalt, with philistine verve, the narcissistic and narcotizing values of consumer capitalism: status, wealth, accumulation, style, celebrity. Small wonder that the O.J. Simpson trial, one of the most sensationalized events of the twentieth century, received more network coverage than any story of the past decade except for the Gulf War; or that the networks devoted nearly twice as much time to Princess Diana (197 minutes) in the five days after her death, as was devoted in comparable periods to the deaths of John Lennon, Elvis Presley, and Princess Grace, combined.[44]

Recent years have seen the revamping of shows such as *Inside Edition, American Journal,* and *A Current Affair,* with more emphasis on serious journalism, such as investigations of political scandals and consumer fraud. But if this new breed of tabs has gone upscale, mimicking the conventions and techniques of news shows while remaining essentially sensational, network news—in a more complex and competitive environment since the emergence of CNN, C-Span, and other cable and satellite outlets—has slid downscale on a converging arc toward tabloidism. A typical emblem of this convergence was CNBC's eager hiring in 1997 of Geraldo Rivera—the talented erstwhile investigative reporter who became the very symbol of trash TV, and who now aims to earn back his dignity along with $6 million a year.[45] Tabloidism in the mainstream media ran rampant during the 1998 runup to the impeachment of President Clinton, creating a media climate in which pornographer Larry Flynt could break news with the exposure of personal lapses by political figures. But it would be foolish to see the tabloid trend as peaking there; doubtless further delights await us.

It has long been commonplace for local news departments to focus on violence and sensationalism ("if it bleeds, it leads,") while ignoring white-collar or organized crime (unless shots are fired) or serious process-oriented stories, such as the statehouse or the city council, or investigations. In 1998, a Los Angeles station interrupted a cartoon show to cover the breaking "story" of a man committing suicide on a freeway. Such sensationalism partly reflects TV's inherent structural difficulty in covering processes, abstractions, or trends without dramatic objective correlatives; but it is also a conscious effort to maintain ratings through an inflationary spiral of ever more shocking visual fare.

Such mutually reinforcing pressures, intensified by cutbacks in network and local TV news departments in the 1980s, have led to more sensational and superficial (and what many consider shoddier, less accurate, and more herd-oriented) news reporting, and the manic pursuit of scoops and ratings rather than clarity, balance or depth. News executives have discovered the profitability of cheaply produced, sensational news. Stories, as well as sound bites, have gotten shorter, as the news hole has shrunk to make room for more ads; there is more emphasis on graphics and glitzy production techniques, and the hyping by stations of their own reporters as trusty, warm personalities and a happy family. It is an environment that encourages frantic emulation of competitors and punishes patient, enterprising, or investigative reporting. Andrew Heyward, the president of CBS News, sums up the results as well as anyone, identifying the "seven daily sins" of network news: mutual imitation, oversimplification, predictability, artificiality, laziness, cynicism, and hype.[46]

Along with the decline of hard news there has been a parallel drop in public affairs programming. Documentaries, the best of which tend to be costly, probing, controversial, and challenging to the status quo, have virtually disappeared from the networks. On public television, documentaries are subject to the economic and political hurdles alluded to earlier. The failure to insulate public television from those pressures is one of the signal failures of American liberalism.

For liberals, however, these various interlocking barriers to progressive values and messages—institutional, cultural, economic, journalistic—are just the good news. In the world of telepolitics, the left faces a more basic problem than the polemics of Limbaugh, the corporate ethic of the networks, the philistine media culture, the narcissistic isolation of the average viewer, or the hurdles it faces, compared to the right, in getting its voices funded and on the air. The TV lens itself is indentured to a way of seeing and mediating the world that is inherently punitive to liberalism. That lens, and not just the corporate domination of electronic media, or the narrow perception of a liberal media bias (or the powerful countercurrent induced by that perception), is the challenge that television poses for progressive politics. The left, in fact, has nothing to fear but television itself.

Shouting Heads: The Language of Television

In teaching us a new visual code, photographs alter and enlarge our notions of what is worth looking at and what we have a right to observe. They are a grammar and, even more importantly, an ethic of seeing . . . the most grandiose result of the photographic enterprise is to give us the sense that we can hold the whole world in our heads —as an anthology of images.
—Susan Sontag, "In Plato's Cave," *On Photography*

Things in motion sooner catch the eye
Than what stirs not.   —Shakespeare, *Troilus and Cressida*

1 · *Television and Mediation*

Most forms of human communication are complex compared to, say, semaphoric signals or animal communication. They are complex, for instance, insofar as they have multiple, invisible, ambiguous, or unintended meanings. The sheer range and diversity of television's messages, social functions, and effects make it a subject of bewildering complexity, and social scientists have debated it for decades. Omnipresent in our lives, television is our main link to the world beyond our immediate milieu, and it transforms both realms. Its sheer pervasiveness, operating for several hours a day in most American homes, makes it difficult to compare with other media or with unmediated activities; even outside the home, it is hard to find a bar or airport lounge that is not TV-equipped. We can even watch while bowling alone.

Given its multiple dimensions—action and motion, speech and sound, lighting and setting; objective representation, subjective narration, and "mindscreen" (dream, memory, fantasy, or other products of a narrative mind)—the analysis of television and its kindred medium, film, is a vast enterprise. This does not mean that audiovisual production always reflects conscious or rational decisions that match means and ends; nor does it entail corresponding subtlety of thought or emotion on the part of the viewer, or a complicated value system in the communicated message. But in purely analytical terms, the grammar of television comprises a vast repertoire of audiovisual parameters, techniques, and devices. Thus, to assess its political influence alone—much less other spheres of impact—would arguably require the joint insights of most of the disciplines devoted to human behavior and values. The purpose of this discussion is not to catalogue that universe or give an exhaustive account of television's idiom, but rather to sketch some of its prominent structural features: the characteristic ways it communicates. In the process, a seemingly contrary pattern will emerge: for all its technological and social complexity, television's main systematic effect on human thinking is that of simplification.

The complexity of televisual communication begins with an obvious but exceedingly pregnant fact: television mediates, in ways that differ generically from other media. That is to say, TV—like any medium—is a unique conduit of information, with its own "language," and not a mere spigot of reproduced experience. It encodes experience into particular formats of stories, phrases, and images. Even when seemingly uniquely faithful to experience, TV, like other media, does not deliver experience itself (and even immediate experience, as we know, can crucially falsify the world, e.g., through distortion, omission, or imperfect recall). Rather, it provides an encoded simulacrum that we generically call information.

Television mediates, moreover, in two subtly related ways. First, it provides a certain kind of picture of the actual experience that the camera records, subject to the technological and commercial limitations that comprise the medium's distinctive language. Second, it mediates in a different sense: providing a certain kind of picture of reality as a whole, and affecting the general texture of human consciousness. Here we will examine how television mediates in the first sense. Later, we will consider the broader sense in which television reports and alters reality.

In mediating (in either sense) between "reality"[1] and the viewer, television alters that which it purports merely to convey. Some such alteration is, in fact, endemic to all communication: whether verbal, symbolic, visual, or otherwise, communication is an encoding and decoding process (and almost by definition a decontextualizing one) in which minds share information, but never in exactly the same form—which would literally require a shared mind. (In a sense, television is a nationally shared mind, but one that only functions in the receiving mode: a distributor of shared perceptions and experience.) Representation is mediation; and mediation, of any kind of information, involves transformation, distortion, and decay.

Mediated experience, in other words, can never perfectly reflect or replicate direct experience. More than just a faithful stenographer of visual experience, the TV camera has its own persona: a set of habits, predispositions, compulsions, and aversions that are rooted in its technological and commercial parameters alike, and affect its selective and editorial functions and the decisions of producers, directors, and editors. Such mediation can be understood at various levels of complexity; the more complex the level, the more it is seen to involve change between the original and the "shared" result. This will prove to be of direct relevance to the role of complexity in politics. But before looking at those broader issues, we need to examine more closely the particular ways in which television mediates: the language it speaks, and how that language makes some things easier to show or say than others.

2 · *The Surrogate Eye*

In comparison to other media, television's communicative repertoire is both miraculous and banal: multiple streams of audiovisual information, mostly representing ostensible realities (or realistic fictions) beyond the immediate domain of our subjective experience. In many respects, those image streams are useful and important; the "immediacy" of mediated experience external to our own—the internalization of it as our own—makes television a unique conduit of information and entertainment. To rely exclusively on print media would be to stunt our potential knowledge of the world—whether of a snowstorm in the next county, the depletion of the Brazilian rainforest, or world history; and that adumbrated knowledge would seem even more incomplete given the expectations that television has cultivated in a bare half-century.

Even its ardent critics concede that television is predominantly a medium of entertainment, not of learning; it would seem vain to hope that it might do more (or less) than mediate, i.e., that it might actually transport experience to us, making it literally our own to ingest intact, like ordering out for pizza. In time, TV or its computer-based equivalent may achieve greater immediacy or "telepresence," for example, by using virtual reality techniques to digitize the relevant perceptions of an actor, reporter, robotic camera, or other surrogate, and conduct them to an audience (each viewer helmeted in a shroud of electrodes) in a form indistinguishable from direct experience, whether of a distant battlefield, ball game, courtroom, or bedroom. But even if television could do that, it would still be a selective mediator; and even if it could replicate consciousness more fully, it would not be our own consciousness.

In their classic analysis of a televised MacArthur Day parade in Chicago nearly a half-century ago, the sociologists Kurt and Gladys Engel Lang showed that the TV camera is far from being a perfectly neutral, accurate, and all-seeing eye.[2] It structures events to create order, sequence, and drama; and it produces "reciprocal effects" as events are structured to fit the contours of television. In this sense, it is not an indiscriminate eye, but one that is limited by its own particular needs and economies.

As the Langs demonstrated, these various TV biases raise interesting questions about the Roshomon-like nature of mediated reality, and which among the various perspectives (or what combination) generate the most authentic experience of an event: that of live spectators, subjects, mediators (TV producers, directors, editors, etc.), or audience. Rather than follow that tangent here, we might simply observe that the organizing and condensing functions that impart coherence and sequence to events are necessarily simplifying functions. They are not necessarily more or less real than immediate experience; they may be both, or may be "differently" real, much as we may learn about reality from a novel or other work of art that relies on certain types of artifice.

In its mobility and versatility, the TV camera frees the viewer from remaining at a fixed position and distance from the subject. Yet, like the human eye, it is limited in its range of motion, how fast it can move, and how long it can stand still. Indeed, one of the camera's compulsions is that it "wants" to see motion in its field of vision, or to shift to new fields (due, among other things, to its much smaller visual field); or to shift its perspective on a scene, changing either camera angle or distance to reveal new things or simply to alleviate monotony. Up to a point, it can substitute action for movement, or vice versa. Documentaries, for example, use slow zooms of still photographs to offset their static nature.

Conversely, a more active subject requires less or no camera movement. But movement and action—or at least the illusion of action—are what the TV camera craves; a news bite or a single scene of a *Seinfeld* episode may consist of only a few seconds of elapsed time and one or two spoken lines. And the essential and obvious characteristic of action is that it involves visible change. It is not about understanding the world but modifying it (and the perception of it); not about static states, abstractions, or factors that are remote in time or space, but about transforming one immediate situation into another.

As an "omniscient" narrator, the camera also has enormous range and latitude. It can literally hurdle boundaries of time and space that the human eye cannot. Hence, it can produce representations (and thus forms of consciousness) that ordinary human experience cannot achieve by itself. It can't outthink us; but it can see more and further, and share the result: as Irving

Pichel surmised in a pioneering article, it is "free from most of the limitations [of] human sight . . . it goes where no human eye could possibly go. It moves according to laws, if any, which apply not to the human eye or the human consciousness but to itself."[3]

One paradoxical consequence is that televised experience, particularly of public spectacles, offers an alternative to direct experience that is both altered (if not downright falsified) and enriched. As a surrogate eye, it is typically the only practical means of experiencing an event—the alternative being to experience something else entirely. Watching a ball game on TV is not a uniformly better (or worse) experience than going to the ballpark; but thanks to the camera's magnification and diversity of perspectives, it affords a richer and more complex visual diet than the single, fixed perspective of the fan in the stadium. The same is true for live vs. video experience of theater and performing arts, nature programs, and other forms of spectacle. It is easier to go to the ballpark than to travel to Washington to witness a presidential news conference, or to Africa to glimpse the wild kingdom. But it is easiest of all to stay home and watch TV.

For all the camera's versatility, however, it is also severely limited on a more global scale, or when reproducing more complex events than particular spectacles fixed in time and space. For the most part, what TV reports as "the news" is comprised of such complex events. In this context, the TV camera's salient flaw is that

it can only look one way. If a story is happening in several or many places at once, TV will see only a little piece of it. It is ill-prepared to tell us about social trends, nonvisual events, or highly dispersed activities (such as a guerrilla war or multiple election campaigns). Further, it forces news to bend to its technological needs. . . . TV shows us what's easy for it to see and not what's important for us to know.[4]

3 · *The Grammar of Television*

In performing its diverse mediating functions of informing, entertaining, and peddling, television simplifies the world. It does this for two general reasons, which are closely related, and which ultimately converge on the screen itself. One is television's technological structure as a mode of communication. The other is the medium's commercial basis, which impels it to be entertaining in the broadest sense of audience attraction and retention. TV commercials don't just sell soap; they sell our attention to sponsors. We, the audience, are the product. Thus, its governing imperative is not to inform or even in the strictest sense to entertain, but to keep most of us watching by strenuously avoiding the risk of our boredom or confusion.

In practice, it is hard to distinguish the "purely" technological features of television from the commercial factors that codetermine its structure and content, or to isolate the conscious and unconscious programming and editorial decisions that reflect those constraints in shaping the final product. This is no accident, but rather a synergy of content and form. The structure, pace, rhythm, and content of TV are joint functions of its technical and commercial parameters. Programming input and production "through-put" decisions that adhere to the structural contours of the medium generate an output that attracts more viewers, and for longer, making the audience itself a more attractive product and yielding higher advertising rates.

This synergy has an important political concomitant. The political advantage that television confers on the right, and the corresponding burden it imposes on the left, have both commercial and structural origins. The sound bites of a Limbaugh, Novak, or McLaughlin clearly appeal to conservative viewers and listeners. But they also hold the attention of moderate, independent, or politically disengaged viewers more successfully than the arguments of the left. Because they hold attention and ratings, they thrive. Shouting heads and ideological food fights may be bad political discourse; but they are great television, and so, without intending to, they privilege conservative messages.

The structure of the medium, or what I am calling the "grammar" of television, comprises a family of conditions and characteristics—specific capabilities and limitations—that govern what gets communicated and how.[5] Strictly speaking, these conditions of televisual language are extrinsic and not intrinsic, but only in a trivial sense: in theory, television can, and occasionally does, opt only to convey, for example, written text (like a book or newspaper), or sound without video (like a radio), or still photographs. But clearly the medium's potentials are more fully realized when it conveys the full audiovisual package of moving images and sound; if those potentials are ignored for more than brief excursions, the audience will defect to another channel. Television doesn't compete with radio or print, but with itself. Thus, for all practical purposes the grammar of television can be considered structural and endemic to the medium, rather than a language of commerce. These defining conditions and characteristics comprise a dense web of related and overlapping features:

1 · First and most obviously, television is an *audiovisual* medium, and not merely a textual, graphic, or auditory one. In fact, it is highly averse to text: reading more than a few sentences

on a television screen, even when the text is scrolling, is impractical and physically demanding of the viewer. A television is not a book—although computers, TV, and print media are converging—just as watching television is not the same as (although it can closely simulate) experiencing a live performance or a spontaneous conversation. Television tolerates verbal communication, sound effects, and music; but pictures and images, and simple speech, dominate. It is, as the Greeks would say, essentially ideographic (focusing on individual, unique persons, events, or things) rather than nomothetic (focusing on general laws that subsume individual cases). Or as Graham Knight explains,[6]

Words move from the general to the specific; they come to the particular situation already formed, loaded with the baggage of previous use, an accretion of denotations and connotations. Audio-visual images move from the specific to the general; in the first instance, the image is always an image of a particular situation, which then attracts and evokes more general associations of meaning. Because of this, the image appears as a more realistic representation; it seems to capture the situation from within itself rather than through the external application of language. This is, in part, why television is often seen as a more accurate, less biased news medium than the press, despite the more obvious subjective presence of the reporter, anchor, and news sources, especially in tabloid television news.

2 · Television is an essentially fluid, *kinetic* (if not hyperkinetic) medium, capable of instantly and incessantly changing the subject—the content of its flow of images; and to a great extent

it must do this, and must compress time, to keep us watching. Like most human consciousness (and unlike still photography, which is more like memory than immediate experience in that it freezes time and motion), television is anchored in motion and time and is therefore fundamentally about change. And because it is not about random change, it depends on pacing and narrative structure to guide and sustain its forward momentum in time and retain the attention of its audience.

Here again there is a direct political corollary. The sheer pace of television, and its acceleration of the political process, militate against a progressive agenda by stimulating what Austin Ranney calls "The Fast-Forward Effect," a demand for "quick and final solutions to complex and intransigent problems."[7] This structural impatience and short-term focus of TV, always hurrying to get on to something new, favors the limited agenda of conservatives and the quick fix over the more far-reaching, structural, and long-term goals of liberals. Moreover, the failure of short-term policies leaves a general residue of public frustration and skepticism about the solvability of social problems and the efficacy of government. On the TV treadmill, we are caught in a perennial cycle of dissatisfaction and disillusionment as quicker, cheaper solutions fail to solve intractable problems that require patience, vision, and tolerance of complexity.[8]

3 · Third, because we are wedded to the immediate flow of sense-experience that the camera records as our surrogate eye and ear, TV is essentially narrative and *episodic* rather than thematic or analytical in character. It can show and tell, but is best at showing; unlike the written word, it cannot readily escape its own immediacy in the here-and-now to examine, define, deconstruct,

question, infer, deduce, analyze, hypothesize, suggest relations among ostensibly remote entities, or glide across different levels of abstraction:

> The written word . . . works through and so promotes consistency, narrative development from cause to effect, universality and abstraction, clarity, and a single tone of voice. Television, on the other hand, is ephemeral, episodic, specific, concrete and dramatic in mode. Its meanings are arrived at by contrasts and by the juxtaposition of seemingly contradictory signs and its 'logic' is oral and visual.[9]

4 · Being episodic and narrative implies that television is fundamentally *linear*, i.e., the moving image tells a story over time. It moves in one direction, seldom doubling back, and the viewer cannot edit or control the pace or direction. (Even videotape affords only the limited capacity to freeze, replay, or fast-forward). For the most part, TV can maintain only one narrative stream at a time, or jump between narratives. The split screen is only a limited exception, serving mainly to juxtapose two parts of a single narrative, such as physically remote speakers in a common dialogue, a pitcher and base runner, etc.; in general, it is hard for TV to depict two or more things happening at once. Whereas written narrative engages the mind in projecting its own internal images, audiovisual narrative is literally a single-channel projection of public images, which the viewer follows in visual lockstep and remembers more or less faithfully.

5 · Being linear and episodic, television is also persistently (if not always profoundly) meaningful and orderly. In a broader sense it may be socially, intellectually, or morally vacuous; but it is never disorganized, incoherent, or empty, except when a sta-

tion goes off the air. A random half hour of TV news or entertainment is invariably more structured than a random half hour
of life; any mediation implies a form or degree of structure. This
orderliness is partly reflected in the fact that we bring to TV a set
of more or less precise expectations, which are rarely upset. For
all its attempts at securing our attention, TV hardly ever surprises
us. For that matter, its emotional climate control is such that it
seldom elicits extremes of pleasure, displeasure, or shock, and
never equals the extremes found in real life. We watch it neither
for those extremes nor to rest our minds and emotions, but to mas-
sage them within reliable and narrow limits of stimulation.

6 · Perhaps most importantly, TV (like the human eye) has a
deep structural bias toward appearances and *concreteness*—
immediacy in time and space—and against generality or abstraction. It is wedded to specific "scenes": the relatively minute units
of experience with fixed, precise coordinates which (unlike larger
themes or events such as human evolution, merchant banking,
Islam, or World War I) can fit in the camera's lens at a given
moment. The more complex and abstract a question, the more
resistant it is to television. As Sander Vanocur said of the declining audience for network TV news after the fall of communism,[10]

> It's not necessarily true that in all cases a picture is worth a thou-
> sand words. A case in point: What is now going on in Eastern
> Europe is just as interesting, though not as dramatic as the events
> of the past year; it just takes a different, more patient approach
> because the pictures available are not so compelling.

Television excels at depicting clear, discrete, highly localized
events, and especially brief or dramatic ones that catch the eye,
rupturing the ordinary flow of occurrences: crime or visible

pollution, highway accidents, the effects of a hurricane, the
NATO bombing of Belgrade, or a refugee camp. It is less adept
at, and hence less disposed to consider, questions that range over
broader expanses of time and space (unless condensed symbolically): root causes and long-term effects, context and environmental factors, abstract ideas or arguments, generalities,
evolutionary change; the social implications of pollution, highway
safety, hurricane preparedness and response, or the larger context of the NATO bombing—such as the history of the Balkans
or the peace negotiations at Dayton and Rambouillet.[11] In sum,
while news stories highlight the superficial and the dramatic,

> Underlying causes and actual impacts are little noted nor long
> remembered. Administrative activity—technical, complex, undra-
> matic, but often with significant effects—is ignored. Politics, not
> government or public policy, is a defining aspect of news worth
> [and] much news alternates threats or potential threats to the secu-
> rity of audiences with reassurances, often resulting from the re-
> actions and responses of public officials, who claim that help is on
> the way.[12]

In a similar vein, Roderick Hart observes that,

> An old theological principle applies: The immanent drives out the
> transcendent. By offering us so many matters to contemplate, tele-
> vision makes it hard, or profitless, to find the connective tissues.
> Television makes us atheoretical, just as it makes us ahistorical. It
> invites us to dwell in the moment and nowhere else. And that is
> where cynicism resides as well.[13]

7 · A particularly common form in which television con-
cretizes is the human form: it *personalizes*, focusing on—and

often exaggerating the importance of—individuals (heroes and villains, freaks, clowns, and celebrities), who typically seem unaffected by broader social forces; and on small groups, such as families, friends, enemies, love triangles, news teams, etc. This is reflected in how TV fosters a spurious sense of intimacy, a superficial and one-way proximity, between viewers and iconic figures: politicians, preachers, movie and TV stars, athletes. Conversely, it de-emphasizes more complicated, abstract, or ephemeral entities such as groups, institutions and associations, social movements, traditions, trends, public taste or opinion, or complex, ambiguous, or growing characters. TV characters, as Todd Gitlin writes, "need to encounter obstacles in society; and by the convention [of television] obstacles have to be personified. Structures rarely exist; culprits do."[14]

8 · Closely related to these biases toward concreteness and personalization are television's propensities for the *dramatic* and the *conflictual*; indeed, these are overlapping descriptive categories. TV personalizes human interactions, dramatizes them as conflicts (arguments, courtroom drama, police and military standoffs), and freights them with violence. Except when creating artificial suspense, it favors the specific, the rapid, the conclusive; it celebrates the extrovert and mocks or ignores the introvert. The most dramatic and exciting subjects, for mass audiences, are the extremes of human behavior: sex, violence, and athletic prowess.

9 · A further corollary of this orderly, hyperactive, microcosmic angle of vision is that television is essentially *partitional*: it is given to segmentation and sharp distinctions of thought and image and averse to connections and syntheses. Every program, scene, and frame has a precise beginning and end; the week, the

day, and the hour are divided by scheduling boundaries. As noted earlier the "eye" of the camera is in some ways more optically limited than the human eye; and the screen itself occupies a small, well-defined portion of our visual field. Again, this is simply to say that it condenses and organizes experience in contrast to how we experience it directly.

Converse to all of these grammatical characteristics of television are its blinkers and aversions: to ideas, explanations, contexts, remote causes or effects, and to anything abstract, remote, or nonvisual. Here again, it is useful to begin by looking through the camera's eye. It is most averse to two broad categories of things. One is stasis, including not just the absence of motion but also of sound or images (silence and darkness). Like nature, television abhors a vacuum. The other aversion is to action that is ambiguous or chaotic. In other words, television insists strongly on narrative simplicity: that something always be happening; that it happen relatively quickly; that it be more or less obvious to the viewer what is happening; and in most cases, that only one thing be happening at a time, with specific causes and effects. It's not much more than we expect of our immediate experience, as opposed to the more fertile and expansive realms of the heart, the imagination, or the inquiring mind.

In sum, by emphasizing the singularity of places, events, and people, television celebrates site, spectacle, and personality. The results may be vivid and informative, but they almost invariably reproduce experience in a simplified dimension. That dimension focuses inordinately on people and objects and simple acts; on the status quo rather than alternate futures or complicated causal histories; on sensation and appearance, not the richer realities shaped by thought as well as perception. Hart's point about the immanent driving out the transcendent can now be put another way: compared to other forms of human communication, television is highly and artificially *focused*. Through its monocular lens, we see the world in small, isolated fragments, with little depth, background, or conceptual framework; but we see it with a beguiling clarity, and in most cases it is only thanks to that lens that we see it at all.

4 · *The Uses of Symbolism*

Because TV traffics mainly in scenes and images that are highly localized in time and space—and in words that must condense their messages to accommodate the medium's visual dimension and severe time constraints—it is also an essentially symbolic rather than a discursive medium: one that, in the broadest sense of "symbolic," compresses meaning. Symbolism, of course, is a large and complex subject, and the term itself is a slippery one. A few general points are relevant to this discussion.

First of all, symbolism compresses meaning by encoding it; thus we are using the term here to identify verbal or visual signs that are more connotative than denotative: i.e., they convey meaning broadly and by convention rather than (or as well as) narrowly and literally. The American flag is an obvious example, as are any words or images, including emblems, objects or props, physical settings, colors, etc., that acquire freighted connotations; symbols may also be encoded in live or dead individuals, statues, architecture, actions, ceremonies, or other conventional tokens of meaning.

Symbolism in general reflects our thirst for (nonliteral) meaning, and an implicit sense of its potential complexity: "Human consciousness," writes George Gerbner, "seems to differ from that of other animals chiefly in that humans experience reality in a symbolic context."[15] We read images not only literally, as the camera does, but also figuratively, relating specific images or messages—the White House, a weather map, a man-in-the-street interview, a buzz word—to more general phenomena, and the general to the particular. Paradoxically, what is most highly localized or literal (e.g., a hammer and sickle) can also be most densely symbolic, redolent of meaning in a broader context that is unspecified but presumed to be understood by the audience. The very specificity and literalness of TV images—such as Monica Lewinsky embracing Bill Clinton—endows them with symbolic importance.

Second, while symbolism is often a complex process, its communicative function (especially in the context of politics and mass media) is to simplify. Literary or artistic symbols may elicit complex thought or feeling, inviting us to interpret or to delve below surfaces; but commercial and political symbols tend to have precisely the opposite purpose and effect. They bypass the critical faculties and invite us to stop thinking, appealing to emotion more than thought, and often simple emotions of attraction or repulsion. The American flag evokes patriotism, not the moral ambiguities of patriotism, or the possibility that such ambiguities may coexist with patriotic fervor.

Symbolic discourse requires deconstruction to be fully understood, a process at which television is inept. Thus, while complex, it functionally simplifies; and (as with television in general) analysis may even reveal that it simplifies in complicated ways. This is because the power of symbolism rests in its not being analyzed or deconstructed by its intended audience; the power is largely in the encryption itself.

"Symbolic interpretations," writes J. Bourdon,[16]

> help to understand the world, while (and because) the question of their value as truth is suspended by the individual. They are unanimously believed to be true without ever being analytically dissected and compared with the world.

Thus political and commercial messages are rife with symbols, and political symbolism in particular is the natural handmaiden of polemic. The Reagan Administration perfected the use of political symbols, and the manipulation of the news media—and especially TV —in using them, in effect turning news stories into free political ads. The Jesse Helms ad depicting a hand receiving a pink slip, with a voice-over implying that the man's job was given to an African-American, was both crude and effective. Such symbols fail when they are sufficiently clumsy and transparent that the media (sooner or later) make an issue of them, as in the Helms case, or Michael Dukakis' tank ride. (It is ironic that the news media focused on Dukakis's failure to use symbolism, and hence the media, more deftly, while George Bush's not-so-subtle symbolic messages were viewed as more effective, a self-fulfilling prophecy.) Again, understanding effective propaganda, such as Ronald Reagan's staged news "events" and "photo opportunities," or Bush's visit to a flag factory or his Willie Horton ad, may involve sophisticated reasoning; but the import of symbolic speech is precisely in how it bypasses such analysis in the short run.

While symbols carry meaning by the truckload, and are often top-heavy, they cannot do the critical work of dissecting their own freight or comparing it to other semantic cargo. Symbolic images or words may refer broadly, but they do not analyze, argue, reason, or explain. They cannot compare or assess arguments, weigh facts, or locate the point where common truths give way to moral, aesthetic, or other normative judgements. Symbols inhibit inferences, deductions, elaborations, or critical challenges; they ignore or conceal ambiguity, irony, contradiction, nuance, distinctions, or a sense of the brittleness of absolutes. As such, they are hardly useful tools of critical or analytic thinking: on the contrary, they typically encode meanings that are vague, visceral, implicit, remote — or even in some cases virtually taboo, as with the swastika or the Confederate stars and bars.

Symbolic communications may be intended to transport us, as in art; to entertain (songs, stories, and narratives have wider meanings, and jokes are often densely encoded); or to get us to buy or believe something, in ways that nonsymbolic discourse cannot. The failure to decode them is the easier and, even with works of art, sometimes the appropriate response. (A poem, as Archibald MacLeish said, should not "mean" but "be.") But while we might scan a poem or stare at a painting all day, it is harder to decode the fleeting images in a kinetic medium. It is easier to take them at face value — which is to say, as emotionally resonant tokens with broader meanings, and ideal tools of uncritical polemical argument.

5 · Sound Bites Man

Television's structure is audiovisual, kinetic, episodic, linear, orderly, concrete, personal, dramatic, partitional, and symbolic. This is not just a random assortment of descriptive features of the medium, but a family of closely related and overlapping characteristics that filter and shape its messages. A final grammatic feature is that television is essentially *fragmentary*; it atomizes information, breaking it down into particles. As Susan Sontag has written of still photography, it "reinforces a nominalist view of social reality as consisting of small units of an apparently infinite number. . . . " On television, as in photographs,

> the world becomes a series of unrelated, freestanding particles. . . .
> The camera makes reality atomic, manageable, and opaque. It is a
> view of the world which denies interconnectedness, continuity. . . .
> Photography implies that we know about the world if we accept it
> as the camera records it. But this is the opposite of understanding,
> which starts from *not* accepting the world as it looks. . . . Strictly
> speaking, one never understands anything from a photograph.[17]

This atomizing process is epitomized by television's proclivity for the sound bite. Indeed, the very term 'sound bite,' drawing an analogy to the basic unit of computer data, is revealing of TV's mosaic character. According to the Harvard researcher Kiku Adatto, between 1968 and 1988 the average political sound bite on evening newscasts of presidential campaigns shrank from forty-three seconds to nine.[18] The increasing commercialization of TV news, writes Adatto, "led to further emphasis on entertainment values, which heightened the need for dramatic visuals, fast pacing, quick cutting, and short sound bites."[19] Among other things, the faster pace of commercials has generated pressure, especially on news programs, to increase their pace and excitement accordingly.

Rooted in cruder forms of mass communication, such as political and marketing slogans, the modern sound bite doesn't just shape how the news is covered. It alters the very character and definition of issues and events; the organization and behavior of media personnel, legislators, candidates, consultants, and lobbyists;

"It's the economy, Stupid"

the content of speeches, TV appearances and news conferences; and the outcome of elections and of legislation.[20] The sound bite has evolved largely in the context of news, public affairs programming, and political advertising, and it is reasonable to surmise that those genres have the most direct impact on viewers' political thinking. But the term applies at least as much to commercial advertising, and in various degrees to other kinds of programming as well (most obviously MTV). Thus, while news and political and commercial messages epitomize the constraints of television's grammar—and news represents television's most direct confrontations with reality—the present discussion nevertheless applies to television as a whole.

While they may conceal complex ideas or stories, sound bites are nominally simple and atomized symbolic messengers. They are scaled to the size and weight of slogans and images, not of rational arguments or complex narratives, in which claims can be logically scrutinized and factually weighed and counterclaims considered. Sound bites, in short, reflect television's broader propensity to compress, atomize, dramatize, and symbolize. They are the medium's natural spawn.

A sound bite society, in which slogans and images supplant arguments and ideas, favors certain kinds of claims and values and certain modes of communication. Thus, for example, unmediated public discourse, with its potential to challenge and analyze—the paradigmatic democratic activity since the time of the Greeks—is dismissed as "talking heads." Instead we have the politics of zingers. This denigration of serious conversation and argument isn't merely capricious; it reflects a powerful bias (though not a rigid imperative) of the medium. Writers and producers seek audiences' attention through action, drama, and lurid shock appeal (typically violence and sex), delivered in bite-size chunks so as not to exceed viewers' presumed attention spans or force them to think. Politicians strive to conform to that style. The more sound bites predominate on television, the simpler, more artificial, and more theatrical and tabloid political discourse becomes.

If serious conversation and text represent two contrasting modes of communication to the sound bite, there is also the disanalogy with art. In most artistic symbolism — in painting, music, or architecture, for example — the size of the smallest message unit, whether a brush stroke, brick, musical note, or other element, bears little or no correlation to the complexity of the whole. If anything, the opposite is more often the case: the larger the units (e.g., the monotonous steel and glass of a skyscraper, or the vast rectangular sheets of color in a Rothko painting), the simpler the whole, at least to appearance. Why is television different? One reason is that sound bites are not in fact irreducible and homogeneous, like single slabs of steel, blobs of color, or musical tones. Rather, they are — like poetry — essentially compressive and symbolic, condensing and encoding larger stories, ideas, situations, or emotive messages.

Unlike poems, however, sound bites are not designed to be scanned, savored, or contemplated. In theory, they can be unpacked to reveal more complicated meanings (or the lack thereof). But as noted earlier, they tend by design to discourage such analytic unpacking. More generally, sound bites and symbols decontextualize. They don't interact to form larger and more complex wholes, like the lines of a poem or the columns of a Greek temple. As ostensibly self-contained reflections of social reality, they do not invite, but replace, connective acts of the mind.

Thus it is no surprise that along with the decline of political discourse into sound bites there has been a parallel decline in public interest and awareness; the generations raised on TV are the first in America to be less well informed than their elders. The dismal state of civic knowledge was noted in the late 1980s, for example, in the National Assessment of Educational Progress; a 1990 Times-Mirror poll found that Americans in various age groups "know less and care less about news and public affairs than any other generation of Americans in the past 50 years."[21] The same report cites these US Census Bureau figures: between 1972 and 1988, voting participation declined by more than a quarter among eighteen to twenty-four-year olds, from 50 percent to 36 percent, while remaining constant, and higher, for older people.

According to the Times-Mirror study, "Sound bites and symbolism, the principal fuel of modern political campaigns, are well-suited to young voters who know less and have limited interest in politics and public policy. Their limited appetites and aptitudes are shaping the practice of politics and the nature of our democracy." The report concludes by noting "the ultimate irony . . . that the Information Age has spawned such an uninformed and uninvolved population." More recently, Howard Kurtz has observed that " . . . in early 1995, only half of Americans could identify . . . Newt Gingrich as speaker of the House, while 64 percent knew that Lance Ito was the judge in the O.J. Simpson trial." Likewise, "After the first one hundred days of the [1995] Republican Congress, polls showed that six in ten people still were not familiar with the Contract for America," despite extensive media coverage.[22]

"[I]t is no secret," adds Christopher Lasch, "that the public knows less about public affairs than it used to know. Millions of

Americans cannot begin to tell you what is in the Bill of Rights, what Congress does, what the Constitution says about the powers of the presidency, how the party system emerged or how it operates."[23] Lasch traces the decline of public knowledge amid a glut of information to the cult of journalistic objectivity propounded by Walter Lippmann, which denigrated opinion and conceived information as something to serve elites rather than to provoke general public debate. Although Lasch's distaste for the cult of objectivity is well placed, in one sense he may have overestimated its influence: the age of information has also become the age of opinion, as reflected in the proliferation of op-ed pages, talk radio, call-in shows, highly opinionated TV talk shows, and similar fare on the Internet. Perhaps the problem is deeper and more complicated.[24]

6 · Summary: The Language of Television

The "grammar" of television — codetermined by its structure and commercial imperatives — shapes the content: what it is disposed to see and what it ignores. Conforming to that grammar, television's audiovisual vocabulary is grounded in the immediate, the visible, the dramatic, the personal, and the emotional. TV likes action and dislikes thought. It favors conflict and spectacle, and disfavors ambiguity, irony, and analytic or abstract thinking; loves violence, and detests rational argument.

TV excels at changing the subject: shifting across time and space in the blink of a frame. It is better at showing the status quo than change, ideals, abstractions — whatever is remote or nonpresent. What enters the camera's lens is the status quo, up close, in isolated fragments. It thrives on sudden, simple, or contrived change: actions or conflicts that are either fictitious or vastly simplify actual change in the world. Gunfire is more telegenic than gun control; jail doors clanging shut are richer visual and symbolic fare than prisoner education—as well as appealing to the conservative belief in simple and forceful solutions to social pathologies. In contrast, subjects involving slow, subtle, or complex change are much less telegenic: evolving or ambiguous conflicts and negotiations, education and research, conferences and committee meetings, child care and job training programs.[25]

Richard M. Nixon was right when he said, "For the press, progress is not news—trouble is news."[26] As a byproduct of its focus on the immediate, the dramatic, and the concrete, TV news emphasizes problems (and especially short-term or breaking crises) over solutions (and especially long-range ones). In this respect, it reflects and amplifies a tendency of democratic politics in general that is punishing to liberalism: namely, the emphasis on immediate, symptomatic issue eruptions and their proximate causes, rather than root causes; on quick fixes rather than far-sighted policies; on the manifest over the latent; and on the economic rather than the political marketplace as an arena of resolution.

A symptom of television's systematic focus on the trees rather than the forest is its affinity for violent crime (which is more visible than white-collar crime or systemic social problems that may contribute to crime); this in turn makes crime more visible (the "Mean World" syndrome), even when the rate of violent crime nationwide is dropping dramatically.[27] Even telegenic events— crimes, accidents, scandals, riots, protests, demonstrations—are invariably more complicated than the images that flow across our screens suggest and frequently have long prehistories and forward-looking solution paths that elude the screen altogether.

Out of this grammar emerges a broader pattern, or system of patterns, in the overall language of television. Socially binding activities and complex, future-oriented processes, such as those involving peace, growth, education, cooperation, community involvement, and family harmony and dysfunction, resist or elude the camera. Complex and diffuse social problems, such as the intractable and interconnected pathologies of poverty, dependency, violence, illiteracy, drug abuse, and teen pregnancy, are likewise viewed only from the perspective of isolated "trees."

On the other hand, specific persons and events, especially dramatic ruptures and socially fracturing activities—war, crime, natural disaster, competition, immediate physical or emotional conflict—are inherently telegenic. An economic crisis can be symbolized in terms of its effects on an individual person, family or town; but the causes of an economic downturn or a dysfunctional family are more elusive and remote and at best can be represented via symbolic episodes. Television can show an emblematic tree falling or an unemployed logger, but it cannot as easily assess the trade-off between logging jobs and old growth Oregon forest; or as Jerry Mander puts it, "Cutting down redwood trees is better television than trying to convey their aura or power."[28] TV can depict a war more easily than its causes and consequences; an act of love, or a killing, more readily than a pregnancy, or the experience of rearing a child; and so forth.

In sum, what is simple, fragmented, short-term or localized plays well on the tube; what is compound, integrated, long-term, or general, does not. Symptoms are telegenic; preventive measures and complex solutions involving the long view, the broad context, the underlying pattern or the root cause, are the bane of television and all electronic media—and the hallmarks of modern liberalism. Television is naturally dissociative and not associative; contrastive and not comparative or analytical. It focuses, with what Pierre Bourdieu calls "structural amnesia,"[29] on what passes before the camera's lens from moment to moment: on the manifest, and not on the latent or emergent; on personalities rather than issues; on the sudden and not the gradual; the obvious and episodic and not the subtle or thematic. Television favors individuals and small groups over larger collectivities, and heroes or villains over complex, eccentric ditherers: Kojak over Hamlet. TV prefers social breakdowns (natural disasters, crime, wars, riots) over the social causes and effects of such events, which elude the camera's eye because they are not reducible to the visible. It is a versatile and sharply focused surrogate eye, but a myopic one.

For all of these reasons, television speaks a simple and reductive language and systematically banishes what we might call its "antilanguage": the universe of deeper and more complex discourse. That antilanguage invokes relationships between the immediate and the remote; between appearance and reality; between certainty and doubt, ambiguity, or ambivalence. It explores the cognitive domains of continuity and causality, of contexts, patterns, and systems, of synthesis and interdependence; it doesn't shrink from the process of abstraction, the strategic separation of meaning from particular points of experience, which is intrinsic to all human thought and language.

Such simplification makes TV a handmaiden of conservative values and messages and a hindrance to the more complicated values and messages of liberalism. Indeed, as we shall see, simplicity is (for better or worse) the epitomic principle of conservatism, and complexity the soul of liberalism. It may then seem more than accidental that television's increasing domination of the political culture has coincided with the resurgence of American conservatism, and the eclipse of liberalism.

Video Games: Television and Reality

■

You're beginning to think that the tube is reality and that your own lives are unreal. . . . In God's name, *you people* are the real thing; *we're* the illusion.
>—Howard Beale, character in Paddy Chayevski's *Network*

[S]urely one of the most visible lessons taught by the twentieth century has been the existence, not so much of a number of different realities, but of a number of different lenses with which to see the same reality.
>—Michael Arlen, "Some Notes on Television Criticism"[1]

1 · *The Medium and Its Message*

In addition to the language of television—the characteristic channels and vocabulary of its information stream—there is another, related level at which TV mediates human awareness. This is what we might call its phenomenology: how that objective stream of messages interacts with subjective viewers to shape our overall sense of reality, as compared to, say, reading, holding a conversation, or witnessing a live event. Here again, the relationship of form to content, or medium to message, is central. Marshall McLuhan was right about this much: the television medium profoundly influences the message. But that doesn't mean we can conflate them entirely or that "content" is irrelevant. And while the message may also reciprocally influence the language, it does not shape the technology itself. At least in a narrow sense, that technology is a given, a cultural artifact that precedes the messages. Let's begin, then, with the safer assumption that medium and message are interconnected in a complex causal web, and that at least some of those patterns of interconnection can be discerned.

Television's impact on our sense of reality is an extension, on a broader scale, of its language. But we are now considering not what is intrinsic to the medium proper (in terms of how television works or how programs are produced) but rather what is intrinsic to the viewing experience, and how that experience frames viewers' perceptions of the world. This broader gauge will afford a more panoramic picture of how television mediates human consciousness, and how, in so doing, it creates a simplified picture of the world—one that can even be a shrewd and informative counterfeit.

Again, this is not an indictment of television for perjury: I am not suggesting that the medium could do otherwise, or that it systematically lies. In fact it tells and shows us important things. And in important ways, TV's picture of reality is technologically determined; indeed, any form of mediation, including speech, the written word, photographs, motion pictures, etc., "subverts" reality by conveying it in selective and limited ways. *All* mediation, by definition, involves some form of decontextualization; no medium or mode of communication is perfect or omniscient, and neither is the human mind.

However else we may conceive it, television is first of all, literally, "seeing from a distance"—a system for selecting and transmitting images en masse, within particular technological, cultural, and economic constraints. It is a cornucopia of the visual. But what else? Some of the more complex and radical arguments claim that social reality and human consciousness are, in effect, media constructs. Without going that far, I will suggest that television plays games with reality and appearance; and those games, while themselves complicated, render a picture of the world that is artificially simple and enslaved to appearance.

An obvious dimension of television's relentless bias toward appearance is the premium it places on visible and cosmetic traits—physical appearance, demeanor, eloquence—as against the less visible qualities of character, the force of ideas, or the integrity of arguments. With its limited attention span and aversion to abstract thinking, TV celebrates the narcissistic values of consumption and instant gratification. The language of television, as we have seen, is the language of immediacy and appearance, of the here-and-now and the self.

From a still broader perspective, television erects a parallel universe: a mimetic suburb of reality that at once simplifies the world, blurs the boundaries of the real, and covers its tracks, obscuring its own complicating role. Sometimes the tube is a brilliant visual stenographer of the world we inhabit, and sometimes mute, inept, or a clever fake. The resulting picture of reality accords with conservative principles in two related ways: first, while TV's two-dimensional picture of the world is itself real and important (just as dreams and illusions are real and important), it is different and simpler than what we otherwise experience as reality; and second, in generating that picture it conceals the *perceived* disparities between itself and reality.[2]

2 · *Veracity and Verisimilitude: The Electronic Eye and Ear*

In its simplest and most obvious function, television serves as an electronic extension of the brain, enlarging our range of perception to include remote environments, with particular capabilities and limitations in navigating those wider reaches of experience. Just as we are conditioned to trust our senses in apprehending our immediate environment, we are culturally conditioned to regard visual images—photographic, cinematic, or televisual—as faithful renderings of the world beyond the pinpoint we occupy in space and time. As viewers, we use two of the same senses, sight and sound, that are crucial to direct experience.

However, the TV camera's unique perceptual capacities both extend and (in a different sense) surpass those of the subjective observer. As a surrogate eye and ear, the camera shows us events far beyond our physical presence; and it surpasses us in achieving, through camera and lens mobility, editing, etc., unique effects (such as a zoom or a jump cut) that the human observer cannot. Thus, to call the camera a surrogate eye is a bit misleading; it is an extraordinary eye, with magical abilities to glide across time and space—which is one reason why we find it so mesmerizing. It does not render the viewer omnipresent or omniscient; but in its unique mobility and multipresence, vaulting one through space and time with a power and speed that are literally superhuman, television "absolves [the viewer] from the claims of deixis, of existing at one place and at one moment."[3]

Even in its very fidelity to appearance, television is subversive of reality. Its vocabulary of images is recognizable from our own lives. Those images are not just an accessory to direct experience, but an important reservoir of mediated experience that influences our memories, dreams, fantasies, goals, and relationships. TV thus legitimizes itself as a visual surrogate by providing us with pseudo-experiences (a term I use without derogation) that are otherwise unavailable to us. For example, a viewer may have absorbed vivid images of Hawaii from *Hawaii 5-0*, as well as from news stories, films, commercials, and other sources; on the other hand, she has been to Jamaica, but cannot recall any images of Jamaica from TV or films. Because video memories compete with real ones, she almost feels as if she has been to Hawaii and not Jamaica, rather than vice versa.

More generally, television competes with and usurps experience. It is an immense cultural subdivision: the Levittown of American attention and leisure time, a vast ghetto of consciousness entered and exited at will. It is compellingly similar to, and yet, due to its functional, technological, commercial, and cultural conventions, inexorably distinct from, the rest of the knowable world. It is both a part of that wider world and apart from it; a distortive, and at times downright parodic, reflection which in turn distorts, consumes, and reshapes the surrounding landscape of life. One could just as easily substitute "television" when Roland Barthes says, "The photograph is a victim of its superpower; since photography has the reputation of literally transcribing reality or a slice of reality, no one ever thinks about its real power, its true implications."[4]

Because of its multisensory character, and its flow in real time, television (and especially live TV, with its authenticating immediacy) projects a unique verisimilitude; in this sense, watching it is remarkably like watching a live event (or nonevent). This superficial fidelity to the human senses imparts a strong simplifying bias: in appearance, TV images are indisputably truthful and familiar. What we see on *Hawaii 5-0*, or even on *Star Trek's* starship *Enterprise*, is not a netherworld but an extension of our own.

"Reality-based" police shows, such as *Cops* and *Rescue 911*, present another kind of disparity between reality and appearance:

realistic slices-of-life, abetted by selection of dramatic situations, shaky-camera documentary style, and other effects. But as such, they also reflect a narrow, ground-level enforcer's eye view of crime and criminal justice; and, produced with police cooperation, they tend to condone official arrogance and brutality, while ignoring the social context, mocking the presumption of innocence, and editing out (or causing police to self-censor) the worst excesses.[5] According to one scholar of television violence, Sandra J. Ball-Rokeach, the police shows "desensitize the audience to the fear and the emotion. The fictional police dramas are sometimes more 'real' because they give you that context. You get a much more subtle understanding of character instead of just action."[6]

The more complex one's interpretation of TV's mediating functions—and one's conception of objectivity itself—the more limited, selective, and even distortive such mediation becomes, and the greater the disparities between the apparent and the real. Those limitations and distortions include the spatial and temporal boundaries imposed by the medium, and its technical and commercial aversions to context, abstraction, causality, and reasoning. But they also include television's ways of framing reality in a broader sense.

The apparently simple technological process of delivering a remote event to our living room is in fact mediated at many points: in the design of the medium (camera, studio equipment, TV receiver); and in the production, transmission, and reception (the producers' and sponsors' boardrooms; the writers' desks and the director's chair; and the eye, ear, and mind of the viewer.) Naturally, that process does not begin with a single, objective event, but is experienced differently by each observer. Events, a philosopher might say, are complex enough without the tints and curves of television's lens.

Thus, as noted earlier, television is most compelling and veracious when depicting activities that are highly contained in time and space: spectatorial human and natural dramas and confined events. It is at its best, in other words, when focused on the spot and the moment—on scenes, or "microrealities," where there is the least discrepancy in the subject itself between reality and appearance—since it excels at appearance. TV excels at reporting space shots, news conferences, monologues, one-to-one interviews or dialogue, interpersonal conflict, sports, or the courtship rituals of gorillas: events that are, or appear to be, entirely self-contained within the camera's range. It is much weaker in portraying ideas or complex events, such as wars, general trends, or historical or social movements, where the images demand more symbolic interpretation and extrapolation by the viewer. In this sense, the less meaningful an event is—or at least, the fewer latent, submerged, or unobvious meanings it contains—the better suited it is for television, in that the least distortion will occur. The camera is an extraordinary eye, but only an eye, not a mind.

3 · *For and Against Reality: Continuities and Discontinuities*

This exceptional close-up verisimilitude arguably has conflicting effects on the viewer's location of him- or herself in the world. On one hand, coupled with certain social and psychological conventions of viewing, it confers on the medium great authority as a source of perceived truth, irrespective of the actual constraints on its ability to convey accurate and complete information. It beguiles us into an uncritical trust in its completeness and veracity as a simple window on reality, while ignoring the ways in which it chooses, frames, and tints that window. We "see" the ball game, news conference, war, or political crisis as if we were at the scene, and often better.

At the same time, however, there are other structural and environmental factors that, without compromising the authority we invest in TV, subtly distance us from "telereality." Electronic consciousness exists within a defined web of visual and temporal boundaries, marked by frequent and abrupt shifts, which instantly relocate our attention in time and space, unlike anything in ordinary experience: not just changes of scene (as with film), but also from one show to another, with commercial interruptions, news breaks, and so forth. Time and space are partitioned into precise segments, whereas real time and space are more fluid. Our control over when, where, and what to watch—and the simple fact of turning the TV set on or off—are at variance with the rest of everyday experience. Also, our expectations of programming content are different and more reliable than those of everyday life. TV is almost always predictable. We choose particular programs knowing in advance that we will be informed, entertained, frightened, amused, outraged, and so forth. In the television world, by and large, "cars do not break down. Convenient parking spaces are invariably available."[7]

Moreover, as noted earlier, it is one of the great cultural ironies of television that while it focuses on the eternal human polarities of merger and destruction, it also, in tacit conspiracy with its audience, systematically falsifies and disguises those behaviors, sanitizing them to conceal the true realities of sex and violence. We vicariously "experience" the extremes of intimacy, athletic exertion, and violence without incurring the actual risks and rewards of gunplay, romance, or of hitting a home run or striking out. Even the most sensational of these depictions are devoid of the true horror of violence, the pleasures and perils of love, the toil of thinking, or the burdens of conflict, decision, and commitment.

In these and other ways, TV land is an idealized counterpart of the real world which both manages it for us and comfortingly distances us from it. It is organized into preconceived genres of experience, neatly divided (at least to appearance) between fact and fiction and according to established genres—soap opera, game show, sitcom, crime drama, news—among which we are free to choose; Arbitron and Nielsen closely tabulate those choices, and marketing departments use focus groups to track how we respond and why. The TV world is edited, classified, scheduled, segmented, and stocked with known and uncomplicated characters, familiar settings, rigid contextual boundaries, and reliable expectations. We don't expect to see a murder on *Cheers* or *Frasier* or a sex scene on *Nightline*. We know, if not what is going to happen, at least what *kind* of thing is going to happen. TV draws us into that world, and we mentally inhabit it, forming habits, opinions, aversions, and allegiances within it; yet it remains at a safe and permanent remove from our immediate life experience. We think of it as "the real world," perhaps even when consciously aware that the world is a far messier, more complicated, less predictable place.

Other important discontinuities between television and direct experience relate to the viewing process itself. An obvious one is TV's linearity: in reading or conversation, one can pause, double back, refocus, sift, edit, and evaluate as one goes along; but TV offers an unarrestable stream of images, usually in the form of a coherent narrative, a forced march of consciousness. And it is essentially theatrical: with rare exceptions, such as

C-Span, most programming is highly mediated at the editorial level, and there is little time or room for critical distancing except on the fly.

Some of the environmental factors that distinguish television from direct experience are obvious. These include the differences in appearance and function between the TV set and surrounding furniture; as a source of moving images and sound it stands out, connecting us to the outside world and to various simulacra and imaginary worlds. Its very physical presence is an invitation to something nonpresent: it is a phosphorescent rabbit hole for escaping reality, and we are Alice. Another dimension of discontinuity is the physical boundary of the screen itself, which is more confining than the human visual field. Television gives us the world in a box—not the world as such, or the world as we see it through our front window. A third kind of physical discontinuity is participatory: the limited freedom of the viewer to switch the set on or off, or to change channels, as we choose between our own unmediated consciousness and electronic alternatives.

These disparate factors, I suspect, reinforce an unconscious or semiconscious sense of detachment between the viewer and the viewed: an alternately thankful and wistful sense that none of this is happening or could happen to us. "The visual man," wrote McLuhan, "is the only detached human being that ever lived on this planet. . . . Only the electronic environment permits a total encounter with the discontinuous and the disconnected."[8] Such subliminal distancing may not discredit, in our minds, the accuracy of a news report or the plausibility of a sitcom plot; but it keeps the world subtly at bay. As Jim says to Alex in a 1981 episode of *Taxi*, "Hey Alex, you know the great thing about television? If something really important happens anywhere in the world, night or day, you can always change the channel."[9]

Yet, despite all of these discontinuities, television is so pervasive and visually credible that in many ways it effectively merges with the rest of experience. On the most mundane level, in its sheer ubiquity and high viewership, it blends almost seamlessly into our daily lives. We are so accustomed to the "seams"—the technological parameters, conventions of programming and scheduling, etc.—that we scarcely notice their artificiality. They are so obvious as to become unobvious. The TV set is among the most fully domesticated of machines. If the dishwasher doesn't work, we can wash the dishes by hand; but the radio is a poor substitute for a nonfunctioning TV set. Choosing to live without one is not just a casual choice but a bold and unusual lifestyle decision. If we give up TV entirely, life may seem more "real" in that we are not exposed to so much mediated visual information, but at least at first, it doesn't seem normal. Television is the norm. Through TV and radio, writes the philologist Mario Pei,[10] "the modern generation has constructed for itself a dream house. . . .

> The borderline between the two and transfer from the one to the other are often reminiscent of what happens when we wake up from a dream: For a time, however brief, we are uncertain which of our two contemporaneous experiences is the real one. . . . The more we become addicted to the news media, the longer and more labored the transition and the more difficult to distinguish the borderline.

Thus, television is not simply "apart from" or "next to" the world; the relationship is more problematic precisely because the two realms are contiguous and outwardly similar, and shape and influence one another. "While not separate," observes Barry Seitz,[11]

> the televised and the untelevised are different from each other. . . . Emphasizing this difference does not . . . depend on granting one of these two terms some ultimate priority. Both are productive, both inform, constitute, and determine each other.

Having naturalized television, we routinely ignore the differences between direct and viewed experience despite their obvious dissimilarities. We forget whether we heard something on TV or in actual conversation or (perhaps more briefly) whether we've been to Hawaii or Jamaica. We habitually accept what is on screen as not just an accurate representation of the immediate scene (which it normally is within limits) but also as a complete, unselective report, while ignoring, denying, or overlooking the structural and commercial filters that define, shape, and sometimes even create the event for us. We think of it as life, only divided into channels and shows.

Television encourages this confusion between itself and the world even as it blurs the boundary between experience and mediation; in effect, it appropriates and reshapes external reality. Life imitates TV as political and other news events are staged to attract TV cameras and to appeal to viewing audiences rather than onlookers. Book sales are increasingly dependent on authors' TV appearances; newspapers are redesigned for visual impact, to compete with televised images.

In some ways, the pseudo-reality of television actually overwhelms and occludes other dimensions of experience. Thus, display ads boast of their products, "as seen on TV," to gain added credibility. What Daniel Boorstin dubbed "pseudo-events" a generation ago are conceived, staged, and scheduled to TV's parameters. Its power to communicate presence, personality, and simple emotions and ideas dignifies certain messages in ways they could never achieve in print: an appearance on *Oprah* imparts a public reality to individuals or causes that they could never attain otherwise. And in an important sense, television's version of politics *is* political reality, subsuming the electoral and governing processes much as it subsumes other aspects of culture in a sound bite society. Outside of TV and talk radio (and certain influential print media) political communication scarcely exists. If a tree falls in the political forest but isn't televised, it in effect remains standing.

Television thus confers on its subjects a kind of "hyperreality": we exalt it beyond our own sense-experience. The civil libertarian Ira Glasser notes that his neighbors look at him differently, and with a certain awe, after seeing him on the tube;[12] he has somehow become more important and, at least in his public existence, more real. People bring portable TV sets to sporting events, and stadiums show instant replays on giant screens (who wouldn't want that?) as if "the television screen were more reliable, more true, more real than the field itself." TV, he concludes, "has a magical capacity to wield influence so that, if the very same idea or words come through a different medium, they are not received or perceived in the same way."[13]

4 · *Teleconsciousness: The Synthetic Revolution*

In sum, television simplifies the world both by conflating reality with, and subordinating it to, the shallower world of televised appearance. The camera doesn't question the completeness or veracity of what it sees; it doesn't recognize, much less examine, its own mediating effects. It offers a blinkered, unquestioning consciousness: a narrowing of awareness that, even at its most vivid or exciting, is less like mental concentration than a kind of sleep. Communication theorists identify this as a secondary form of consciousness, or "teleconsciousness."

The differences between teleconsciousness and ordinary awareness (to summarize) are based on at least three related phenomenological effects that television has on information. First, TV nominally (but brilliantly) mirrors the physical and social world we inhabit. What we normally see on the screen is not simply a counterworld—as in the film *Contact* or the more exotic episodes of *The Twilight Zone*—but a highly recognizable (yet mediated, commercially driven, often contrived, and voraciously attention seeking) simulacrum of the one we know. What we see on the screen, unlike out our window, desperately *wants* to be seen. Second, as a limited and selective mirror, TV crucially distorts the world it reflects, among other things by emphasizing, altering, or adulterating certain types of human behavior and situations. To keep our attention, TV must show us the real world, but falsify it without our really noticing or caring.

Finally, because of its ubiquity and apparent capacity to mirror life, TV ultimately disarms us, inhibiting distinctions between reality and fiction. It is so pervasive, mimicking and displacing so much direct experience—several hours of the typical day—that we cannot fully differentiate what we know from TV and what we know from direct experience or reflection; the distinction itself loses meaning, and we don't even try. As tourists, we view the world through the lenses of video cameras. What we learn from our interactions with family, friends, or colleagues blurs with what we assimilate from sitcoms; our sense of history is shaded by the mental images and ideas we form while viewing fictional miniseries and docudramas. TV, as one writer puts it, "encourages us to think of itself as the same thing as living."[14] The ultimate artifact of modernism, it challenges and erodes the very concept of reality.

But it isn't just television's ubiquity or verisimilitude, as a source of both fictional and factual narrative, that alters our sense of reality; it is also the narrative itself. Art at its best, in all forms and genres, plays continually with our sense of the real. Using a plethora of frameworks, stylistic techniques, and devices, it takes us out of our daily experience to wrench, seduce, or guide us into new perspectives, and then returns us to Earth feeling enlarged. But TV is such a relentless simulator (and so inherently disinterested in our sense of what is real) that it does not return us to Earth but keeps us in orbit, so to speak, creating a permanent confusion of realities. Art, in a tacit compact with its audience, self-consciously plays with, distorts, and expands our sense of reality. Television, in most genres, is the opposite of art: it invades reality by stealth and displaces the real, both in our minds and in our daily lives.

"The root of this unfortunate problem [of confused realities]," writes Jerry Mander, "lies with the fact that until very recently, human beings had no need to make distinctions between artificial images of distant events and life directly lived."[15]

As a hybrid of reality and artifice, teleconsciousness is a unique product of audiovisual media. Until the nineteenth century, human experience was largely confined to the immediate and authentic reports of the senses; the great exceptions, of course, were the written and, since the fifteenth century, the printed word. But in the past hundred and fifty years, photography and electronic media have engulfed us with sensory images of remote experience, creating what G.R. Funkhouser and E.F. Shaw call "a quite different perceptual world from that in which human perceptual capabilities and the social institutions of Western civilization had evolved." The new media, and above all television in its ubiquity and multisensory character, radically altered human perception: *"Introduced into one's sensory envelope, they appear to extend it beyond its natural limits"*[16] [My emphasis].

Funkhouser and Shaw list an array of synthetic techniques whereby electronic media artificially "format" perception. These include the alteration of time itself, such as through fast and slow motion and instant replay; "instantaneous cutting from one scene to another"; "excerpting fragments of events," e.g., as sound bites; "juxtaposing events widely separated by time or space"; "shifting points of view, via moving cameras, zoom lenses, or multiple cameras"; the use of music, sound effects, dubbing, and lighting; and computer graphics, animation, and other techniques for "merging, altering, or distorting visual images" or for the outright manufacturing of "events." As a result, to a degree unprecedented in human history, " . . . a considerable portion of our sensory input now comprises . . . synthetic experiences of real and synthetic events."[17]

Accordingly, Funkhouser and Shaw propose a four-fold matrix for identifying degrees of authenticity of experience: 1) real experience of real events (e.g., cooking or tending a garden, listening to live music, holding a conversation, etc.); 2) real experience of synthetic events (attending a sporting event, political rally, or other event in an institutional framework); 3) synthetic experience—filtered by the audiovisual techniques noted earlier—of real events, such as a televised actual occurrence; and 4) synthetic experience of synthetic events, ranging from sitcoms to televised debates and Boorstin's "pseudo-events," tailored for media consumption. Most public occurrences, of course, have both a synthetic and a natural dimension. A baseball game may be played on natural grass, but it is a contrived social event, not a purely natural one. And while a ball game would hardly be the same if there were no fans in attendance, it is also a different kind of event in the television age.

Extrapolating from this matrix, we might say that watching a nature program or documentary is a synthetic experience of a real event, whereas most television content (sitcoms, sports, news, etc.) involves synthetic experience of (more or less) synthetic events. Thus, watching an animal in its natural habitat would constitute the most authentic form of animal-viewing experience, followed by (respectively) seeing one in a zoo or circus; seeing one televised in its natural habitat; and seeing one featured on a late-night talk show. But the value of such a matrix is not so much to rigidly classify events according to how and why they are mediated, as it is to appreciate the complexity of mediation itself, and the tangled web of reality and telereality it creates within human consciousness.

The triumph of telereality is demonstrated with exquisite irony in a 1992 commercial for a Sony Trinitron TV set. The ad shows a Trinitron sitting on the rim of the Grand Canyon; depicted on its screen is the same panorama that forms the actual backdrop. A boy runs toward the TV set, oblivious to the surrounding natural grandeur. Turning back to his parents, he points to the screen and yells, "Hey, look, it's the Grand Canyon!" Though perhaps intended as a wry comment (and evidently based on a 1961

Chevrolet ad),[18] the Sony commercial darkly implies that we would rather watch the Grand Canyon than be in it—even if we could do both at once. As Peter Conrad observes, "We have almost been persuaded not to accredit the reality of anything unless we can experience it second hand, mediated by the television cameras."[19]

5 · *History and Reality*

For some further perspective on television's framing of reality, we might briefly consider some of the problems inherent in how it treats past events through drama and docudrama, documentaries, and as a venue for feature films. The documentary genre, in particular, includes what many would consider the medium at its best and most informative. Fiction can also inform, of course, whatever the genre or medium, and at its best conveys important truths; that is why Robert Penn Warren called poetry "the lie we must learn to live by if ever/We mean to live at all." But when history is dramatized through fictional techniques such as symbolic condensation, composite characters, and fabricated scenes and dialogue among actual historical figures, a hybridization occurs: an imperfect (if often successful) marriage of information and entertainment. The results are inevitably at least somewhat deceptive—as are soft and tabloid "news" shows that use "infotainment" to highlight the sensational or dramatize the trivial. The question is not whether such recreations are misleading or false, but who is deceived and how, what are the proper boundaries of dramatic or commercial license, and what critical tools viewers need to be aware of boundary violations.

Other things being equal (which is hardly a foregone conclusion) television is neither an inferior alternative to, nor a counterfeit of, written history or print journalism, but rather an indispensable complement: think, for example, of Ken Burns's documentaries on the Civil War and baseball, or *Eyes on the Prize*, the seminal account of the civil rights era. Spoken words and images are in some ways uniquely effective modes of communication and learning. Besides, learning is a matter of the heart as well as the head: dramatized history can stir and inform viewers and inspire discussion or trips to the library. "Shakespeare," as Mark C. Carnes observes, "by omitting the fact that Henry V slaughtered hundreds of French prisoners at Agincourt, perhaps failed as a historian; yet we do not propose that *Henry V* be stricken from the literary canon, or that some committee of earnest historians undertake its revision."[20]

At its best, television can both approximate and augment the reality of subjective experience; and therein lie both its virtues and its flaws. The more localized, dramatic, and visual an event—the more reducible it is to a "scene" or visual scenario—the better the job of TV. Visual evidence, when available, also contributes immeasurably to our understanding of discrete events in the past.

Having the Zapruder film of the Kennedy assassination is surely better than having no visual record at all. But it doesn't follow that one could understand that event solely from visual images, or that being in the crowd at Dealey Plaza when it occurred would have yielded a better understanding of it. While a crucial part of the visual record, the Zapruder film clip—a quintessential sound bite etched in American consciousness—depicts a mere fragment of an event that remains, in the view of many, unfathomed. Visual evidence, for all its prima facie authenticity, is not the only kind of evidence (and neither is the printed word always adequate or infallible). The past wasn't wholly unknowable before the advent of mass media, and it isn't wholly knowable now.

In considering television as a vehicle of historical knowledge, the same structural imperatives apply to it as to other TV genres; commercial and technological imperatives—the limits and language of visual narrative—can restrict and distort understanding. Historical biographies, for example, are typically melodramatic, personalized conflicts between heroes and villains. Disdaining ambiguity and uncertainty, they exaggerate the power, charisma, and personal virtues or flaws of their subjects.[21] Even the best documentaries tend to simplify history by emphasizing wars and personalities, or what historians call the "great man" theory of history: the individual, the immediate, the tangible, the violent. Via archival film clips, we can "witness" the Japanese attack on Pearl Harbor, but not the complicated political and military context that produced it. Human voices and conflicts are important; but other elements that enrich historical narrative resist the screen: interpretive depth and nuance, causality and context, ideology and controversy, obscure human motives, group dynamics, influential ideas, and broader historical forces and conditions.

Like TV in general, televisual history contains other pitfalls besides those relating to commercialism and entertainment values. The abstract nature of the printed word requires the forming of mental pictures, which must be processed actively and rationally. It does not visually relocate us on the scene, or provide a definitive image or stream of images, but compels a process of interpretation and assimilation that is conceptual, not literal or photographic; it is more participatory, summoning the brain to think.

Visual information is essentially more passive and less cerebral. Pictures overwhelm words; they have a superficial wholeness, an appearance of totality and credibility that makes them harder to erase, revise, or replace with images of the mind's own conjuring—even when we are consciously aware of their contrived or unrepresentative character. We might call this the "indelibility effect": striking visual images have a way of embedding themselves in our minds irrespective of completeness or accuracy, and even when, intellectually, we know them to be wrong or synthetic. Pictures have a certain of epistemic innocence: they don't lie outright; they just lie in all sorts of other ways. Paradoxically, it is the very inability of the printed word to impart such precisely fixed visual images that partly accounts for its inestimable communicative value.

Related to this is what we might call the "critical effect." Images are harder to sift, edit, or analyze as we view them. It is easier to evaluate disparate or conflicting textual sources, or to dissociate elements and form an independent interpretation, than to assemble a visual picture from various images given to us. (Images seldom if ever "conflict" in the literal sense, precisely because they are so literal). Hence, there is a predilection to accept what we see as authentic, and most visual images imply such authenticity. However edifying the result, it is bound to be a simpler, not a more complex, picture of the events in question.

TV docudramas, even when relatively accurate historically, are problematic in a further dimension, related to these effects. The invention of characters, dialogue, and episodes inevitably produces a blurring between fiction and fact in the viewer's mind. The problem with docudramas, and historical dramatization generally (including feature films from Oliver Stone's *JFK* to

Schindler's List, Titanic, and *Saving Private Ryan*) is how to weigh the potency of the aural and the visual against such factual and critical hemorrhaging. They may provide vivid accounts of real incidents or characters, yet focus on narrow, atypical, or even relatively insignificant events, both real and imaginary. Whether on balance such historical recreations shed more light or shadow is a murky question, and depends on the critical sophistication of both the program and the viewer. But they invariably render a simpler historical account than can be obtained from a wider range of sources and media, and one more removed from the elusive goal of historical truth (insofar as it is the goal).

While the structure of televised history reflects the medium's simplifying bias, its content messages (like those of TV in general) are not uniformly conservative. For instance, the historian Eric Foner argues that docudramas tend to project "the revisionist view [which] portrays American history as filled with group conflict, racial injustice and threats to democratic institutions." But as Foner further notes (and here again commercial forces come into play), the docudrama tradition is "only selectively revisionist. If racial injustice is an acceptable subject, class conflict is not. The history of American labor is ignored in the docudrama, as is the experience of the immigrant."[22] Obviously, isolated incidents of racial prejudice or social protest are much easier to televise than, say, class structure, exploitation, or segregation as a way of life.

Some forms of audiovisual deception are more readily discernible than others. One example of high artifice is the use, along with interviews and actual film footage, of grainy, black-and-white re-enactments, a technique expressly designed to dupe less sophisticated viewers through spurious verisimilitude: not to mimic reality, but to mimic authentic reproductions of it.[23] Other kinds of inauthenticity, such as anachronisms or improbable locations, are more obvious to most viewers. But artifice in general, and the (more or less obvious) interplay between fiction and fact, is endemic to our visual culture—as it is to literature and "nonfiction novels." All cultures have fictions, and all cultures are based in large part on stories, legends, and myths. Fiction can serve fact, and fact can enliven fiction. The danger is greatest when commerce, not art, education, or collective memory, motivates the fusion.

Needless to say, the ways in which great events are mediated in an image-driven age have become artifacts in their own right, inseparable in public memory from the events themselves. Examples range from the Zapruder film to the recording of the Hindenburg disaster, Edward R. Murrow's wartime radio reports from London, the Nazi propaganda films of Leni Riefenstahl, the defining images of Vietnam, or Bill Clinton's embrace of Monica Lewinsky captured on video. History, since the emergence of mass media, has come to include the chronicle of those media and those sound bites.

It is difficult for even the most critical viewer to keep direct and mediated experience entirely distinct—that is, to withstand the critical effect. Our imperfect understanding of the world is based on an incalculable range of stimuli from disparate sources, including our direct experience (which in a large event such as a battle or a political convention is invariably fragmentary and deceptive); what we see, hear, and read in various media; and our imperfect recall of all of these inputs. Televised images, in their attention and fidelity to "scenes," whether fact or fiction, and their capacity to blur the two, are at once (and in varying degrees) accurate and indispensable, artificial, fragmentary, and misleading. Knowledge of the past or the present can never be complete; nor does simplification always decrease such understanding. The pursuit of historical truth is asymptotic: an approachable but ever-receding ideal. But we can apply critical standards to ensure that we are approaching it, and not moving in the opposite direction.

Thus, to call television a limited and volatile instrument of news or historical knowledge is not to deny its informative potential, or the reciprocal limitations of the written word. We need not hold all media to the same standards of truth, or ascribe to them identical functions. Nor can we hold TV to the standards of academic history — the ultimate repository of historical knowledge, but one which can also lead to obscure, overspecialized inquiry where, as Simon Schama has observed, "more and more is known about less and less." There is much to be said for engaging a vast audience (as did Ken Burns's *The Civil War*, among others), and no ready formula for balancing breadth of audience against depth of understanding. But as a form of storytelling capable of seizing the imagination and conscience, history can be held to reasonable standards of truth; and television, for all its inclination to intellectual passivity, can be a great storyteller. What it too often lacks is the language, incentive, or discipline to be a wise one.[24]

6 · *Technology and Reality*

A final, fluid frontier between television and reality is the one defined by the onrushing tide of technology. Incipient technologies such as digitization and high definition, or HDTV, promise significant improvements in the TV (or telecomputer) viewing experience, including greater visual fidelity and interactivity. But these emerging features offer no comfort to stubborn reality buffs; in fact, they will only enhance television's ability to subvert, and camouflage its subversions of, the real. High definition, for example, by improving television's scenic fidelity, fortifies the camouflage by further narrowing the perceived gap between appearance and reality. Superficially, this additional credence will be justified; at least, it is not a reason to keep your old TV set until the analogue system is phased out. Like color TV in the 1950s, HDTV makes the "seam" between TV and actual experience less visible, but not less important.[25]

Digitization, whereby computer bits replace celluloid, videotape, and phosphorus as the delivery medium for television's sound and images, is more revolutionary and problematic. With it, the very integrity of visual and sound recording, which formerly implied permanence and authenticity, is thrown into question.[26] For artists, commercial advertisers and graphic designers, political propagandists, and others, the photographic negative has long been merely a starting point for creative mischief, aided by computer-graphics tools such as the Paint Box and the Scitex machine. Using the device known as the "Harry," available since 1987, TV studios have been able to manipulate both animated and natural images. Time-compression machines allow programmers to accelerate the pace of films and TV reruns by up to 8 percent without distortion, freeing up time to put more commercials before an unsuspecting audience. But digital technology extends the capacity to alter or retouch images into a brave new world of almost infinite and seamless manipulation. Not surprisingly, thorny copyright issues have emerged in what is largely a legal terra incognita.

Computer generated imaging (CGI) has already begun to play havoc with the boundaries of reality in feature films, generating images that are perceptually credible but factually impossible, in effect "extending the principles of perceptual realism to unreal images."[27] We have seen long-dead movie stars enlisted in advertising campaigns; and we have grown used to such phenomenological dynamism as the lifelike dinosaurs of *Jurassic Park*, the conversation between President Kennedy and Forrest Gump, or the "appearance" of President Clinton at a press briefing in *Contact*. The realistic images seduce us into perceiving what most (or some) of us know cannot be. (While television currently offers fewer examples, these will no doubt proliferate as feature films, computers, and television programming converge.)

As a result, the presumptive veracity that is the hallmark of the photographic image is no longer immutable; and this breach between appearance and reality will alter and confound the politics of visual information in the twenty-first century. (Perhaps nondigital media will survive as quaintly veracious forensic tools in courts of law or public opinion.) This is just one area—human cloning is another—in which technology has created choices and possibilities that outstrip our ability to draw and patrol the boundaries of moral consensus.

In many and obvious ways, technology expands the envelope of human perception without corrupting it. Aerial and space photography are now mundane, but like television and still photography, they provide images that were previously unavailable to the human eye. At the opposite end of the scale, a film such as *Microcosmos* likewise extends the bounds of the visual by using robotic cameras to show the behavior of small and microscopic creatures: ladybugs mating, caterpillars marching in file, a water spider building an air pocket in its submarine lair, bubble by bubble. Nevertheless, the pinpoint objectivity that has assured the phenomenological integrity of the moving image can no longer be taken for granted. In an electronic media environment endowed with sophisticated techniques for manipulation, and extending to the cybersprawl of the Internet, pictures can lie outright. And given the chance and commercial incentive, they surely will.[28]

7 · *Summary: The Panoptic Fallacy*

On the simplest understanding, television is an innocent mediator: a powerful electronic handmaiden of sense perception that selectively magnifies aspects of reality, expanding and enhancing, but not otherwise altering, human consciousness. On a somewhat more complex view, TV expands the human perceptual envelope in a new dimension—generating, in effect, a new lobe of perceptible reality, while subtly distancing that world from us by projecting it as an alter-world that is more manageable, orderly, predictable, and self-contained and less threatening than the actual one, without creating any boundary problems between those two worlds.

While each of these views makes nominal sense on one level, and has simplifying merit, a third alternative has been suggested here: that television projects a different reality, a false mirror whose boundaries with the world of ordinary consciousness are inherently problematic and incompletely chartable, but can be generalized about. Television, in this more complex view, plays various complicating games with reality. It is neither an innocent conveyor belt of perceptions, a tabula rasa, nor an unreality machine that constructs everything we know, but a medium whose filters and frames variously reflect, simulate, and falsify experience.

The resulting telereality exists in a continual resonating blur with the real: extending, masking, modifying, displacing, and usurping it. The world of images we receive electronically is not independent of direct experience, but in a constant and fluid dialectic with it, creating a kind of double vision in human consciousness. It continually challenges us to keep those worlds distinct, and it does so not on some objective, accessible territory but where we live: in our minds.

That challenge has paradoxical and sometimes contradictory effects on consciousness (which also depend of course on who we are and what and how we watch). Yet while these effects are themselves complex, they do not render our overall sense of the world more complicated. Rather, in its pervasiveness and verisimilitude, TV masks its intricate betrayals of reality. Even in viewing ostensibly raw, live coverage of actual events, we lose sight of the continuous mediation that is occurring and of the uncertain boundaries between the immediate and the mediated. That appearance of all-seeing "realness" is the panoptic fallacy inherent in television.

Television is unself-conscious. It never contemplates the different levels and kinds of reality that the human mind can discern, or its own complicated phenomenological footprint. But let's not dismiss it for being unphilosophical. TV's more serious crime is to seduce us into thinking it *is* the world, when the world is in fact broader, deeper, and more complex than its synthetic reproductions—selected, edited, segmented, labeled, narrated, structured, categorized, scheduled, staged, scored, symbolized, etc.—would suggest. Whether news or entertainment, telereality is infused with simple clarity and meaning, while the rest of reality is shot through with complexity, confusion, ambiguity, and uncertainty.

TV, in short, doesn't just add to or subtract from our everyday awareness but transforms it. Not all viewers are naive or uncritical, and cartoons and science fiction are not the only genres that are patently unrealistic: most of us can distinguish between the forms and rhythms of *Seinfeld* and those of our own lives. But even adults cannot entirely escape the subtle framing effects of news, the apparent verisimilitude of sitcoms or soaps, or the reverberations in our minds and memories between what we watch, for thousands of hours a year, and what we experience.

Television's treatments of historical subjects reflect and amplify these general mediating effects on how we see and understand the natural world. New technologies, by more deftly manipulating visual reality in the service of entertainment or persuasion, and more artfully concealing that manipulation, figure to further undermine our ability to juggle realities. The more games TV plays with nature, and the better it plays them, the more complicated is the disparity, both technologically and in theory, between reality and appearance—and the less we are aware of it. Using ever more sophisticated techniques to mediate, and to conceal the rules of the mediation game, television insists on its own simpler view of the world. As we shall see, that simpler, more appearance-bound world view is also a more conservative one.

Complexity and Ideology

■

Finding the real identity beneath the apparent contradiction and differentiation, and finding the substantial diversity beneath the apparent identity, is the most delicate, misunderstood and yet essential endowment of the critic of ideas and the historian. . . .
— Antonio Gramsci, "Journalism"[1]

1 · Television's Myopia and the Problem of Complexity

All communication simplifies, as an imperfect process of sharing information. In important ways, the human mind is itself a simplifying instrument, imposing perceptual, logical, and conceptual order on sensory experience through definitions, categories, distinctions, linguistic conventions, and the like. Television, as we have seen, further simplifies the world by systematically filtering out more complex modes and dimensions of understanding. TV is not so much "out of focus" as myopically focused on the foreground of ordinary experience: the particular scenes, objects, places, persons, and events that it can depict effectively.

This myopia is discernible at various levels: in the medium's political and commercial imperatives, its structure and characteristic language, and how that language affects the broader conception of social reality. Television, in sum, thrives on action, immediacy, specificity, and certainty. It filters out 1) more abstract and conceptual structures or relationships, including systems (which are relationships that interact over time to produce particular results or to maintain a particular balance); 2) causality, particularly remote causal histories and destinies, evolutionary change, and uncertain or incomplete processes of change; 3) context, which is likewise relational and causative; and 4) ambiguity, i.e., uncertainty of meaning, and ambivalence, or uncertainty of value.

In other words, television's communicative structure, converging with its commercial imperatives, systematically rewards what is simpler and punishes what is more complex. We can now move on to the next part of the argument: that whatever its other merits or drawbacks, simplification epitomizes political conservatism. Accordingly, this chapter will first take a closer look at the concept of complexity, and then relate complexity and simplicity to political ideology.

The ways in which television simplifies, as a pervasive lens on experience, are themselves complex questions. That much would seem fairly obvious and nonparadoxical. But complexity is a notoriously difficult idea, and one that has received scant theoretical attention beyond the realm of pure science, where it remains a highly unsettled mode of inquiry. Even in science and mathematics, no single, all-purpose definition of complexity has been agreed upon.[2] There is at least the threat of a paradox of self-reference here, in that the idea of complexity, even at the level of definition, itself seems ineluctably complex.

In exploring its relation to politics and the media, it will be useful to distinguish several general senses of complexity: a broadly numerical one; a generative or systemic sense, of particular relevance to science and mathematics; and an analytical sense, more germane to questions of communication, social organization, and human values. But I would stipulate at the outset that in making these distinctions, I am using the term 'complexity' in essentially the same way as it is understood in ordinary language, with a meaning that we intuitively grasp and find useful, however elusive a more precise definition may be.

We recognize complexity first of all as a descriptive property term, and therefore a relative one. It would have no meaning apart from its conceptual opposite, simplicity. Intuition and ordinary usage suggest also that complexity pertains to knowability: it identifies something as being neither easily knowable nor inscrutable, but rather, we might say, remotely knowable. Thus, to begin with its antonym: the *Oxford Concise Dictionary* defines 'simple' as "not compound, consisting of one element, all of one kind, involving only one operation or power, not divided into parts, not analysable. . . ." The emphasis is on unity: the absence of internal distinction or differentiation. For example, the color green appears to us as a relatively simple natural property, a range on the color spectrum. In more complex terms, we understand it as a range of light wavelengths, or as a blend of the primary colors yellow and blue.

Likewise, 'complex' is defined as "consisting of parts, composite. . . ." It derives from the Latin *complexus*, denoting "to embrace or associate with." Complexity describes what is (relatively) less obvious, less readily apprehended, and/or contains more parts, aspects, functions, etc. that can be internally distinguished, or externally related to other things.

Common sense and ordinary usage often imply an essentially quantitative notion of complexity. For instance, there is nothing objectionable about the observation that "the greater the number of elements [in one's perspective on international relations] the more complex the perspective. . . ."[3] We intuitively understand that a recipe is more complex when it involves more steps and ingredients; a machine is more complex if it has more moving parts; a symphony is more complex than a sonata; a corporation more complex than a storefront enterprise or a pushcart; and so forth.

Mere quantity, however, does not entail complexity. A greater number of pixels on your TV screen does not make for a more complicated image. Rather, a multiplicity of discrete variables with their own identities or causal inputs, whose interactions produce further effects, comes closer to defining complexity in the numerical sense. At the same time, complexity is not always causal. Some things are logically or conceptually complex (such as the concept of freedom), having more internal divisions or external connections, as distinct from having more complex causal histories and destinies (e.g., a human life, or a flu epidemic).

Visual media tend to be simpler systems of communication than the written word in both the causal and conceptual senses: at least outwardly simpler, in that they convey discrete units of experience. They are not necessarily simpler technologically, or in terms of how they convey information; TV cameras and control rooms are complicated affairs, and so is communication theory. But television generates a kind of information that is clearly fixed in space and time, in a realm of directly observable actions, causes, and effects. Anything on TV, by definition, can be seen; and visual images seldom make explicit distinctions or connections of thought. They cannot literally think for us, or perform analytic functions, as words can. Television can depict an apple falling on Newton's head, but it cannot as readily convey the causal or conceptual complexity of the ensuing ideas in his head.

Complexity, then, is best understood not as a chaos of causal forces acting unpredictably on a given state of affairs, but as multiple causal or conceptual elements acting interdependently.

Most of the things we call "systems" (whether organic or inorganic) are complex virtually by definition: systems of meaning or computation, such as languages, computer programs, or mathematical algorithms; economic systems of production and exchange (or a subsystem such as the stock market); artificial systems such as the game of chess; natural systems, such as the weather; ecosystems;[4] the human body, the brain, or the mind. The globalizing capitalist economies, like the human psyche, are an extraordinarily complex system and fiercely resistant to analysis on television.

Systems are frameworks in which disparate elements interact to produce common but intrinsically unpredictable or hard-to-predict events: a particular chess position, a storm, a book, inflation, bulimia. They are processes of integration, disintegration, and change. As such, they are neither so orderly as to generate readily foreseeable outcomes, nor random, chaotic, or wholly inscrutable. They involve forms or rules of order (natural or artificial) that conjointly generate what humans perceive as progressive levels of disorder or unpredictability. Systems, in other words, are phenomena or relationships that reflect conceptual or logical patterns but are experientially opaque or unpredictable. In trying to understand a system, we are concerned with its causal pedigree and potentials: what is it made of, where did it come from, and what will it lead to? What rules govern its evolution? Thus, the yardsticks of a system's complexity include the range and diversity of identifiable agents interacting in the system, and/or the range and diversity of rules or observed patterns governing those interactions.[5]

2 · *Political Dimensions of Complexity*

Differences over the respective roles and limits of government and the market constitute defining watersheds (or better, "values") of the simpler and more complex political visions. Laissez-faire is a simpler model of society than the welfare state. Arguments about types and degrees of regulation and redistribution of wealth are more complex than arguments against regulation and redistribution as such; appeals for cutting taxes are simpler (not only in appealing directly to voters' self-interest) than arguments for preserving or raising taxes. Self-interest, as such, is a simpler basis for political evaluation than any more altruistic or communitarian calculus. But the contrast between simpler and more complex value frameworks occurs in many, if not all, areas of social thought and policy.

Criminal justice is a salient example. Conservatives advocate simpler approaches based on force as a means of retribution and deterrence ("law and order," more police, harsher sentencing, etc.); liberals stress more complicated remedies, such as rehabilitation and preventive or interventionist measures, which tend, at least in the short run, to be costlier in various dimensions—including money, time, and their more complicated assumptions about social cause and effect. Night basketball may have been a good idea for America's inner cities, but the Electronic Right seized on it and turned it into a sound bite, as a symbol of alleged liberal excess.

Complexity arguments are similarly reflected in educational disputes; and here too, they help to explain why issues seemingly remote from the political barricades may nevertheless be highly politicized. Progressive educators typically advocate an integrated

The realm of foreign policy might seem more ambiguous, since the issues here are not defined in terms of domestic market-related politics and the division of power and wealth. It is an arena of at least relative consensus insofar as shared democratic values and national security are on the ramparts, rather than the specific domestic concerns of liberal or conservative ideology. Sen. Arthur Vandenberg's dictum that "politics stops at the water's edge" thus holds true in a narrow sense. But in fact, debates about America's role in the world are similarly informed by complexity-based ideological differences. Here, the traditional fault line divides a more "realist" view, which conceives national interests more narrowly (and more exclusively in military and economic terms) and an "idealist" one that puts a premium on promoting human rights and democratic values overseas.

Such rights and values, incidentally, are inherently more difficult to visualize or televise (except in extreme and symbolic cases); they seldom make the evening news, and don't directly affect American audiences. Analogously, conservative opinion historically gravitates to the extremes of isolationism and military confrontation, dividing the world into friends and foes of American interests—a view that was greatly facilitated by the Cold War and complicated by its ending. Liberals typically favor subtler and more complex responses, including diplomacy, trade and economic sanctions, peacekeeping missions, and humanitarian aid.[6]

Further baselines of complexity lie in different ways of understanding mediation in general, objectivity, and technology. There are many forms of mediation, motives and tools for shaping and conducting information, and types of realities—objects, situations, events, ideas, relationships—that may be mediated. Nevertheless, we can generalize along the following lines: On the world as it is.[10] They see technology as normatively charged, with the potential to favor, or even create, particular classes of citizens; at the extreme, technologies are regarded as wholly ideological and instruments of domination. On this view, technology is both a source and a product of society's codes and cultures, in which it is deeply embedded: As Albert Borgmann puts it, "the ensemble of technological artifacts immediately expresses and all but enforces a distinctive and morally charged form of life."[11] Instead of simple cause-and-effect, the left postulates a more intricate dialectic of interpenetrating means and ends, form and content, ideas and modes of mediation. Langdon Winner calls this process "reverse adaptation"; Neil Postman observes that, "[t]he form in which ideas are expressed affects what those ideas will be."[12] Means and ends shape one another—and the right's sharp dichotomy between means and ends itself shapes means and ends.

Likewise, to the conservative mind objectivity is a readily available norm, identified with known and shared facts about the world, and a kind of antidote to ideology—or at least to complex ideology. Television, on this view, delivers objective reports of reality; technique—in the broad sense, including every phase of human intervention from the design of the medium to the editorial function—simply contributes to that more or less perfect mirror. To the complexitarian, while objectivity may remain an important ideal, it is a more complicated and elusive one, and of more limited value. It is compromised by principles of selectivity; slanted by technique (again in the broad sense); and so forth. Objectivity must be pursued, but (except in limited and uninteresting cases) can never be fully attained, and, more importantly, cannot be conceived in isolation from other norms of communication. Finally, on the more radical view of the

Marxist or critical theorist, objectivity, outside of certain narrow scientific contexts, is a fantasy or a sham, a spurious attempt to transcend the self and society.

On the simplex view, television news provides uncomplicated representations of social reality, and television entertainment provides more or less independent fictions. But on the complex view, news is not perfectly representational or factual, and neither is fiction purely imagined; rather, both of these electronic realms distort and filter the world within an intricate web of causal reciprocity, each influencing the other. In practical terms, the left is more apt to discern and evaluate the connections underlying dichotomies such as "news" and "entertainment": how entertainment delivers "news" about society, and how TV news adopts the techniques and formulas of mass entertainment.

Similarly, liberals regard an FCC license to broadcast on a band of the electromagnetic spectrum as a complex transaction involving a public trust—somewhat like leasing scarce federal land, but with much higher market value per acre—and involving a dense network of assumptions and regulations regarding property, enterprise, free speech, and the public interest. There may be contradictions or anomalies in that transaction, as some argue.[13] But to the typical conservative station owner, the FCC license is simply a charter to do business, and the band allocation a type of deeded private property like any other.

A further dimension in which a more complex, boundary-crossing outlook competes with a simpler and more logically rigid one is in the status of theories in the social sciences and humanities. Indeed, the traditional distinction between more scientific or quantitative disciplines under the rubric of social science, and normative inquiries in the humanities, has itself begun to fade into a broader intellectual horizon known as the human sciences. On the complex view, theory is not simply a form of knowledge that serves to explain, predict, and control practice, as conventionally understood; as a form of mediation, it also plays a constitutive role in shaping social reality: "Theory becomes not the crowning achievement of an objective social science but rather an integral component of an engaged social practice."[14]

Similarly, scholarly attention to deeper textual and discourse analysis, to the effects or biases of methodology, and to metatheory in general are characteristic of the traditions of Marxists, critical theorists, and others on the left. Implicit in these denser theoretical orientations is a signature of the complex vision: the idea that pristine distinctions, such as between fact and value, and between objective inquiry and normative claims, are logically possible but practically untenable, if not spurious.

3 · *Analytic Complexity and the Geometry of the Mind*

Underlying all of these political and intellectual differences is the complexity spectrum. Whereas conservatives gravitate toward a simpler, more fragmentary model of social and political interaction, governed by fewer, clearer, and simpler rules, liberals bend toward a more complex, integrated, and communal vision, and a more comprehensive and ambitious agenda. Where conservatives emphasize the visible (which television excels at) progressives stress the disparities between reality and appearance, and accordingly, connections, patterns, systems, causes, contexts: phenomena that are unobvious, inobservable, and intrinsically resistant to a medium wedded to immediacy and appearance.[15]

The left and the right, in short, tend toward opposite ways of resolving the post-Cartesian dilemma of reconciling matter—or what we might call the random messiness of experience—and the pristine geometry of the mind. In resolving this primal tension, conservatives (to generalize broadly) characteristically appeal to clear and rigid distinctions and dichotomies, as bulwarks of meaning and intellectual order. Complexitarians pursue a more fluid intellectual balance: not rejecting conceptual absolutes, but seeking to relax and transcend them. On this view, such absolutes are not fixtures of reality, inscribed in the universe (like Plato's forms), but flexible instruments for mapping the shifting terrain of reality. They both reflect and organize experience in a constant dialectical flux and serve as the foundations for more complex calibrations of meaning, much as a painting must begin with the blending of primary colors.[16] Here as elsewhere, the simplex view emphasizes the priority of form over content, while complexity posits a more intricate relationship between content and form.

Ordinary experience seldom requires such analytic probing. We commonly understand what is meant by a *house*, or the color *green*, without examining their definitions or relating them to, say, *barn* or *yellow*. But at higher levels of abstraction, including moral and political discourse about concepts such as freedom, justice, equality, opportunity, and responsibility, the analytic process becomes an important economy of meaning. And such concepts are, by their nature, approachable from standpoints of relatively greater or lesser complexity. Indeed, we cannot help making implicit choices about analytic complexity in treating them; and the choices we make reflect our most basic value differences.

To further explain analytic complexity, a brief digression is in order. Virtually all cognition ultimately involves one of two basic

tion, the nine sitting justices, or the history of judicial review; but it cannot be fully understood apart from its formal and historical relationships to those other ideas.

The tensions between fluidity and formalism, between implicit and explicit meanings, and between distinction and connection, are endemic to all human thinking, because language can never perfectly mirror the interplay of thought and experience. Words and concepts implicitly draw distinctions and connections. But distinctions nominally obscure connections, and vice versa; thus, there are always reciprocal connections and distinctions to be drawn, and competing ways of differentiating and relating the elements of reality.[17] This is accomplished by analytic thinking, which renders explicit what is otherwise implicit.

In organizing our conceptual and moral-political world views, there is a polarizing tendency. On both levels, conservatism is epitomized by simplicity: clear distinctions, isolative and dissociative mental acts, and a primary focus on the self and the unregulated market—in sum, a smaller, neater moral universe, with fewer rights and duties among agents and a less demanding (as well as a less rewarding) social contract. At the vulgar extreme, it lapses into sectarian or tribal hostility toward outgroups defined on national, ethnic, racial, lifestyle, or other lines.

The progressive world view reflects opposite tendencies: toward a more connective, integrated, and systemic understanding of social relationships (whether a system of rights, or of social pathologies, or an ecosystem) and awareness of evolutionary change. It envisions a more inclusive and tightly woven social fabric, with stronger bonds and greater equality among its members. Individuals are seen not as billiard balls, each autonomous and whole, but as fibers in that social fabric of individuals, families, groups, communities, institutions, nations, ideas, and broader social and economic forces, sharing common histories and destinies. In all of these ways, complexity is inimical to the language of television and corresponds to what we have called its antilanguage.[18]

Seen from another angle, simplex conservatism is rooted in the principle of fission. It thrives on partitions, both in the mind and between the self and society. If vulgar forms celebrate exclusion and hierarchy, in more elegant versions those fissures represent important conceptual cleavages, and the insular dignity of the conservative individual. Liberalism inclines toward fusion, but without necessarily ignoring the social and intellectual virtues of fission. Indeed, in its more elegant and complex forms liberalism conjoins the principles of fusion and fission (as it links form and content), seeking to reconcile individuality and community, and distinction and connection, and thus to gain a more powerful grip on the world than is possible with either principle alone.

Clearly these are very broad rubrics, with any number of possible gradations between them. The complex framework presumes to offer a greater purchase on reality, but at the potential expense of simplicity and clarity, and perhaps other intellectual, cultural, or political costs—including resistance to sound bites. Norberto Bobbio cautions against either extreme:[19]

> Those who adopt an analytical approach should never forget that reality is richer than abstract categories, and should continually review them in order to take account of new data or new interpretations of old data; equally the historian must be aware that, in order to understand, describe and order the factual realities that

documents reveal, he cannot do without the abstract concepts which, whether he realizes it or not, are provided by the advocates of analytic judgements.

These contrasting visions form the enduring moral and conceptual scaffolding for the left-right ideological spectrum in democratic societies. Because of the competition between them, announcements of the demise of ideology (or the obsolescence of the terms *conservative* and *liberal* or *left* and *right*) are not just mistaken but in fact naive: we invariably divide along this spectrum. The broadest reason for this is the basic metaphysical (or subconscious) choice between the two frameworks. More specific, but related, reasons for ideological differentiation lie in the persistence of two modern conditions. One is free-market capitalism, which creates differences of economic status, security, opportunities, mobility, and power—in short, divergent political interests. Such class stratification ensures diversity of interests and opinions on wedge issues of equality and wealth. The other condition is political democracy, which allows those divergent interests to be expressed and negotiated.

Given these two conditions, we are able to talk and have something important to talk about. Thus, ideological partisanship is not the ant at the political picnic, as some suggest; it's the meal. Contrary claims often appeal to the values of bipartisanship and pragmatism. But genuine bipartisanship is only possible on a narrow range of highly consensual issues; otherwise it is merely a rhetorical device for suppressing partisan differences. True pragmatism is flexibility about political means; flexibility about ends is opportunism.

4 · *Polarized Thinking and the Agony of Ambiguity*

Complexity does not just involve tolerance of contradictions—the internal distinctions and external connections that nominally afflict stable identities—and the recognition that conceptual boundaries can be porous without collapsing. It also tolerates ambiguity and ambivalence in place of rigid certitude. And here, too, it is both antithetical to televisual language and anathema to the Electronic Right. To become a liberal, Rush Limbaugh would have to change more than his roster of polemical targets; polemics itself is incompatible with uncertainty, ambivalence, and complexity.

"Some have suggested," writes E.J. Dionne, Jr., "that liberals are 'on the one hand, on the other hand' sorts of people."[20] Like most stereotypes, this one overgeneralizes a basic truth: it is more characteristic of complexitarians to equivocate, ambiguate, and qualify, to blend or balance opposites, to look below surfaces; that is one reason why liberals do not have their own Rush Limbaughs. The simplex view is more disposed to see the world in rigidly dichotomous, black-and-white, either/or terms: what Norman Lear calls the "binary imagination."

No one has described this basic cleavage in the intellectual universe better than Primo Levi,[21] who was confounded by the question: "Have we—we who have returned [from the concentration camps] been able to understand and make others understand our experience?

What we commonly mean by 'understand' coincides with 'simplify': without a profound simplification the world around us would be an infinite, undefined tangle that would defy our ability to orient ourselves and decide upon our actions. In short, we are compelled to reduce the knowable to a schema: with this purpose in view we have built for ourselves admirable tools in the course of evolution, tools which are the specific property of the human species — language and conceptual thought . . . perhaps for reasons that go back to our origins as social animals, the need to divide the field into 'we' and 'they' is so strong that this . . . bipartition — friend/enemy — prevails over all others. Popular history, and also the history taught in schools, is influenced by this Manichaean tendency, which shuns half-tints and complexities: it is prone to reduce the river of human occurrences to conflicts, and the conflicts to duels . . . [t]his *desire* for simplification is justified, but . . . simplification itself . . . is a working hypothesis, useful as long as it is recognized as such and not mistaken for reality. The greater part of historical and natural phenomena are not simple, or are not simple in the way that we would like.

As we have seen, the polarity between distinction and connection has various analogues: fusion and fission, identity and difference, oneness and multiplicity, association and dissociation, attraction and repulsion, self and other. The very concept of 'relationship' implies this elemental tension between unity and division; to relate is to show connections between identities transcending the distinction(s) that prompt their individuation in the first place. (Thus, France and Germany are distinct identities, and it would be hard to conflate them; but both are countries, they share a continent and a border, etc.) Similarly, the human mind and interpersonal relationships are in constant dialectic between harmony and tension, dependence and independence, attraction and aggression. "Two variables," writes the psychologist Marion F. Solomon, "influence the course of all intimate relationships."

> On one hand, there is a sense of separateness and autonomy, a freedom of action. On the other is the universal desire for an occasional regression to a state of 'symbolic fusion'—perfect understanding by a loving other ... [f]inding an acceptable balance between these two desires is the dilemma of love relationships.[22]

A similar dichotomy describes the infant's emergent sense of itself in the first months of life, springing from the realization of the mother's separateness. "Judgment," notes the psychoanalyst Donald M. Kaplan,[23] "begins with the recognition that personal appetites are not continuous with the supplies that gratify them."

> There is an inside (appetite) and an outside (milk), and these are separate realms. . . . Cognition is built upon the ontogenetics of subject/object split, which begins with psychological separation from the mother and an appreciation of the mother as a person in her own right.

Television, Kaplan argues, represents a "morbid regression" to the infantile preseparation state that "requires so little judgment and interpretation that it never raises the question of whether it is inside or outside, whether the eye or ear is a distinct sense organ or simply a variant of the mouth; for this reason, experience with the medium must be placed at the primitive level. . . ." In short, it defeats or obscures relationships on all levels—intellectual, interpersonal, and cognitive. Or as Jerry Mander puts it, "Television isolates people from the environment, from each other, and from their own senses."[24]

This is not to suggest that a predisposition to bonding or separation, or to complexity or simplicity, predominates in every individual; and certainly a highly conflicted mind can also be a nimble and subtle one. But psychologists have long observed connections between extreme cognitive rigidity, intolerance of ambivalence and ambiguity, and political intolerance.[25] Rigid thinkers tend to dichotomize the world into black and white, and make quick, decisive, and unqualified black-and-white evaluative judgements. They have trouble maintaining adequate boundaries or thinking in terms of probabilities, cling to immediate experience and rules, and (like television) are averse to abstract or future-oriented thinking. Recent research confirms a strong predictive connection between cognitive sophistication or flexibility and political tolerance, including "openness to new ideas, and willingness to risk uncertainty and ambiguity."[26]

5 · Summary: The Forms and Uses of Complexity

In sum, a family of closely related ideas defines the "complexitarian" framework, in the social-political sphere and in thought in general. First, integration and interdependence on various levels: of form and content, of method or process and results, of ideas and social forces, and of the individual within his or her community and society. Second and third, a commitment to causal and contextual explanations of isolated phenomena, i.e., to understanding how they are integrally related to other phenomena. Fourth, an appreciation for the variances between appearance and reality; and fifth, tolerance of uncertainty.

In the analytic realm, complexity corresponds to the more fluid use of abstractions to isolate meanings, recognition of the logical fissures and fusions that apply to stable identities, and avoidance of black-and-white polarities. The complex thinker preserves those identities while exploring their internal and external relations, and adopts an instrumentalist approach to concepts in general, seeing them as flexible tools of the mind. An opposing family of ideas, with their own intellectual virtues and drawbacks, defines, the simplex vision. These include commitments to particularity and immediacy over abstraction; to conceptual partition rather than integration (and to distinctions rather than connections); to the logical and social independence of phenomena, concepts, and individuals; the identity of appearance and reality; and an aversion to uncertainty, ambivalence, and ambiguity.

Mental acts of connection and distinction, or fission and fusion, are elemental (if not ultimate) constituents of thought. While these twin functions are in principle compatible, linkage and integration are the intellectual signature of complexity and the political left; partition and division, which simplify and schematize, are the signature of the right. Distinctions are the elemental boundaries of meaning at the root of all thought and language; connections are equally important in transcending those boundaries to reveal what they nominally conceal. To distinguish between apples and oranges is a simpler logical act than to discover their common properties, origins, or functions; but both are indispensable. While the simplex framework has the virtues of clarity and obviousness (much as television has the virtue of transmitting vivid scenes), the complex framework has contrasting virtues, penetrating across boundaries and below surfaces to reveal underlying realities of meaning and social organization.

6 · *The Political Spectrum: Formal and Synthetic Visions*

Against this background, we can consider more directly how complexity functions in the political dimension of ideology.

Democracy, in the broadest sense, is based on the principle of political and legal equality among citizens. It consists of the equal right to participate in government and certain correlative rights (speech, worship, assembly, etc.) vis à vis the state: roughly, equality before the law, and in choosing the lawmakers. Although progressives are notably more enthusiastic about extending this principle of equality into areas hitherto governed by the market, such as workers' rights or campaign finance, the narrower idea of democratic citizenship forms the shared constitutional basis for our ideological disagreements. Television's "democracy effect" is its impact, as the major source of public information, on such basic political equality.

While there is a broad consensual commitment to democracy qua political equality, its logical complement, economic equality, is the salient axis of ideological contention.[27] In essence, this axis relates to the distribution of material rewards, as opposed to formal and procedural rights.

On the simpler view, the economic realm lies largely beyond the domain of moral accountability; the libertarian simplicity of laissez-faire is valued over the complexity of redistribution and market regulation. No modern conservative would endorse a return to slavery, child labor, or the twelve-hour work day. But business enterprises are deemed to have fewer if any prima facie obligations to workers, consumers, children, the communities in which they function, the natural environment as a collective interest, or to other affected interests. Indeed, what constitutes an "affected interest" is itself an important point of contention.[28] On the contrasting liberal view, private enterprise does not always promote the common good or respect individual rights; the demands of justice may conflict with the freedom or efficiency of markets; and government must address those disparities, to reduce inequalities of wealth and/or to protect rights that the market would otherwise abridge or threaten.

The ideological spectrum can be understood, therefore, as one between a simpler and more formal view on the right, and a more complex and synthetic one on the left. The two views implicitly contend over how to accommodate the formal and conceptual apparatus of the mind, and of law, to the gritty uncertainties and interpenetrations of the real world. For the right, justice is satisfied by formal political equalities: equality before the law, meritocracy, and so forth. The left, on the other hand, seeks to concert formal and material considerations, or processes and results.

Liberals argue that de jure equality does not equate with de facto equality. This is not because formal equality fails to yield absolute equality of results (an impossible and unnecessary goal); in fact, liberalism endorses a range of distributive principles and criteria as appropriate to different spheres of social intercourse: need, talent, merit or achievement, luck, formal citizenship, and so forth. Rather, formal equality is insufficient because in the real world there is no clear bifurcation between processes and end states, or opportunities and rewards: opportunities lead to rewards and vice versa.[29] Formal equalities, on this view, do not ensure true equality of opportunity; hence Anatole France's noted remark: "The law, in its majestic equality, forbids the rich as well as the poor to sleep under bridges, to beg in the streets, and to steal bread."[30] State laws, we might add, allowed rich and poor alike to pay poll taxes in the segregated South.

Inequality, then, is a simpler goal both in logical and practical terms. It merely involves adhering to a clear (if artificial)[31] boundary between political and economic goods and insulating economic goods from principles of redistribution: i.e., creating a *cordon sanitaire* around the market. Egalitarians have the more complicated task of justifying, and bringing about, off-market allocations, distributing various goods at various levels of relative equality and according to various criteria.

This dichotomy of visions is basic to our political culture—or for that matter, to any democratic capitalist society, in which there is both room and need for open debate about the division of power and wealth. President Clinton—a man of many talents but no philosopher—alluded to it in the summary of his second debate with Bob Dole in 1996.[32]

> This election is about two different visions. . . . Would we be better off, as I believe, working together to give each other the tools we need to make the most of our God-given potential, or are we better off saying, you're on your own? Would we be better off building that bridge to the future together so we can all walk across it, or saying you can get across yourself?

The insistence on concerting formal and material values, among other things to optimize equality, permanently complicates the liberal task; viz., the complex and problematic debate over affirmative action. The conservative has no such chore: political equality is sufficient, and social inequality a tolerable by-product of human competition and differences of nature, luck, drive, and talent. For the conservative, the principle threat to freedom is government itself. For the liberal, government is both a potential threat to certain freedoms and a guarantor of others: freedom from the predations of other individuals and institutions.

Few on the left seek to radically equalize wealth or believe that such an outcome could even be approximated in a complex society. They tend, rather, to support the "third way" of market allocations within boundaries democratically determined in the public interest and safeguarded by active, but not overbearing, government. In other words, liberalism advocates what might be called *dynamic equality*: a level of material welfare—whether in the form of tax relief, income transfers, loans, scholarships, public education, health care, housing, legal aid, etc.—intended not to ensure success, which every citizen must define for him- or herself, but to mitigate the costs of failure and (perhaps most of all) to prevent those costs from becoming intergenerational. Lyndon Johnson stated the case most clearly.[33]

> Freedom is not enough. . . . [I]t is not enough just to open the gates of opportunity. All our citizens must have the ability to walk through the gates.

Adherence to this hybrid principle of equality sharply distinguishes and complicates the liberal argument. It adds one dimension of complexity by pursuing both formal and material principles in tandem, and another in that the redistributive principle of dynamic equality is necessarily open-ended, relative, and self-limiting, whereas political equality, as a conception of the formal rights of citizenship, is simple and absolute.[34] A further complication is the liberal conviction that the two egalitarian principles do not just represent twin social goods, but are interdependent. Again, it challenges the distinction, arguing that, in actuality, the right to vote, speak, or organize is dysfunctional in the absence of basic material goods, such as the wherewithal to learn, communicate, participate, or travel.

Material deprivations discount the full value of citizenship;

equality before the law, for example, means little to those who cannot afford adequate legal representation. In the real world, the liberal claims, form and content, process and end state, intermesh. Normative social theory must observe those distinctions, but must also recognize how they blur in the complexity of the social world. The liberal challenge is to see both the logical simplicity of concepts and the disorder of actual experience, without surrendering either perspective.

Along with the priority of formal equality over result based or synthetic principles, several closely related ideas animate what I am calling libertarian or dignified conservatism. They serve as convenient descriptive markers for a coherent and (on its own terms of complexity-tolerance) compelling argument in the democratic conversation. These ideas include small and decentralized government; the supremacy of the private over the public realm; laissez-faire capitalism; and an autarkic individualism that is reflexively hostile to public enterprise.

Of course there are as many shades and varieties of conservatism as there are of liberalism; but intellectually as well as politically, the common denominator of the right is the simplicity of its social arrangements. That simplicity is rooted in weaker (large-scale) social bonds and obligations; a commensurately smaller role for the state; and a proclivity for clear barriers, both conceptually (Cartesianism), between the real and the ideal, and around the self (egocentrism), the group (tribalism), and the nation (nationalism). Any expansion of that narrow moral and conceptual horizon represents a leftward move on the political spectrum: a move toward greater equality and greater complexity.

Conservatism is dubious of the liberal vision's social webs of value, obligation, and causality. Those complex webs are not necessarily less emotive or more cerebral, per se, and are no less value-laden; but they appeal to different and less egocentric values and emotions. The primary conservative bonds to self and family are simpler and more personal than bonds to more abstract entities such as a community or class; they imply less moral adhesion between the self and others. Private interests (however enlightened) are more concrete than public interests; they have a clear address and are seldom subject to doubt or debate. One may feel a deep attachment to a conception of the collective public interest—and not to the exclusion of the more immediate bonds to family and self—but such other-regarding attachments imply a more complex understanding of one's place in society. Liberalism is defined by its commitment to that understanding.

7 · The Three Equalities

In a broad sense, all of the basic differences between the moral lenses of left and right turn on rival conceptions of equality. I have thus far mentioned two senses: formal equality (on which there is general agreement) and (relative) material equality, on which there is broad left-right disagreement. A third form of equality further distinguishes liberalism from its rivals, in particular from vulgar conservatism, and from the weaker strain of American opinion that surfaces from time to time as a kind of vulgar or militant radicalism. That third form, the most openly contended one in America at present, is equality of dignity or respect, which equates with tolerance: respect for moral, political, or other differences, and for civil debate.

Essential to equality of respect is the ability to distinguish one's own conscience from that of others and to recognize their equal moral standing. This emphatically does not imply moral relativism or deny us the right to make moral judgements, above all in cases where there is palpable injury, whether physical or material, psychological, reputational, or otherwise. But it recognizes a zone of moral silence, of privacy and restraint, where those standards of clarity and consensus are not met.

True liberals, on this general definition, subscribe to all three conceptions of equality; dignified conservatives adhere to two of them: political equality and equality of dignity. The views of their more extreme brethren on the right imply neither dynamic equality nor equal dignity; at best, they share the implicit belief in democratic citizenship that (minimally but crucially) binds American culture and grounds the ideological spectrum itself, from Jesse Jackson to Jesse Helms. At worst, they implicitly endorse social and racial hierarchies beyond those of class that the market generates. Respect for differences of opinion, practices, or lifestyles is a sine qua non of liberalism, and intolerance the hallmark of the vulgar conservative. As a rhetorical gambit, the right-wing accusation of "political correctness" may sometimes succeed in showing liberals to be intolerant or foolish; campus speech codes are a sorry example. More often, the charge of "political correctness" is the voice of intolerance demanding its (sometimes legitimate) right to be intolerant.

Tolerance debates revolve around those social issues—abortion, feminism, school prayer, gun control, sexuality—where simpler and more complex moral codes, rather than economic interests or concepts of economic justice, conflict. The issues evolve over time as levels of tolerance rise in some areas, and new forms of intolerance are exposed by social change. The present roster of social issues has all but eclipsed the foundational ideological debates over political and dynamic equality, reflecting the deep rift in American culture between Christian fundamentalists, for whom morality is rooted in scripture, and liberals and libertarian conservatives, for whom it is rooted elsewhere: in Judeo-Christian ethics; in John Stuart Mill's principle that we should only proscribe those actions that "do harm to others"; and in the promptings of individual conscience.[35]

While liberal tolerance is more "permissive" and less given to dogmatic absolutes, it is only relative insofar as it insists on wider latitude for individual conscience on matters it deems essentially private. If anything, it constitutes a more rigorous standard of individual conduct, notably in demanding forbearance concerning actions by others that do no manifest harm—although what constitutes harm, and who are to count as others, remain in question.[36] Liberalism is likewise more exacting in its trade-off of marginal autonomy for justice and security: it asks us to pay more taxes, to share more public space, whether in the form of national parks or access to education or health, and generally to be, to a greater extent, our brother's keeper.

In its social messages, American commercial television is, on the whole, at least passively tolerant.[37] Unlike talk radio, TV is inhospitable to blatantly intolerant speech, despite the veiled forms propagated by the electronic pulpit; but neither is it always an impressive agent of toleration. TV's gravitational field is toward conformity and homogeneity, and generally offending as few viewers as possible; but it ignores or dismisses, more than it openly condemns, nonconformity. TV offers distortions and stereotypes, but seldom vicious caricatures, of working women, racial and ethnic minorities, homosexuals, political dissidents, and spiritual commitment. I suspect that TV may have a plateau effect here, engendering more tolerant attitudes in some viewers up to its own level, but suppressing higher levels (and perhaps even confirming prejudices); in the same way, it may promote literacy up to its own level among children and non-English-speakers, but discourage higher levels.[38]

8 · The Politics of Causality

A final axis of the complexity spectrum, and one which underscores its relevance to political life, is that of human and social causality. This axis reflects competing ideas of individual responsibility—and has everything to do with our ideological commitments. Conservatives locate responsibility for social behavior more exclusively (and more simply) in the self, which is independent and existentially autonomous: we are fully answerable for our own actions, achievements, and failures. This is exemplified on television by Christian broadcasters' narrow appeals to the self through dramatized salvation stories. Such appeals reinforce (in the words of Sara Diamond) "a worldview that frames social problems—and their solutions—primarily as matters of individual behavior and/or supernatural forces, not as problems to be addressed through collective social responsibility."[39]

Toward the opposite end of the spectrum, the causal framework of the left is increasingly deterministic. This is not the determinism of a single causal agent such as an omnipotent god, but rather the positing of multiple spheres and levels of causal agency beyond the self, in keeping with a more complex and panoramic conception of the moral-political enterprise. The complexitarian individual is subject to a vast web of external influences: other agents, collectivities, social institutions and conventions, environmental and experiential conditions, historical and cultural forces. The human will, values, and our very selves, both shape and are shaped by that wider environment. This more integrated vision rejects the putative insularity of the conservative citizen as an artificial contrivance in defiance of social reality. In these competing causal frameworks, each with respectable philosophical antecedents, are the very taproots of ideological conflict. A brief consideration of that causal debate is therefore in order.

In science, where we test, measure, and predict nature, we are inclined to causal determinism for the simple reason that nature is, on the observable level, manifestly (and almost by definition) deterministic: it is a domain in which, at least in principle, every event has an external cause.[40] Much the same is true of the social sciences, which explore human causes and effects — in the economy, social conduct, or the mind itself.[41] It is no coincidence that the pioneers of modern thought, such as Darwin, Weber, Marx, and Freud, are tacit determinists, whose theories of human behavior implicate causal forces other than the conscious mind. Virtually all social inquiry, and science on the supra-atomic level, presumes that we can identify causes and effects that are distinct from the human will.

Yet, when we consider human values and individual behavior, a reversal occurs. Here, rigid determinism affronts our intuitions; we can't help supposing that we are free agents, causal subjects rather than (or as well as) objects within a wider causal web. Without at least some free will, and concomitant responsibility for our actions, we lose a certain dignity; but more than that, the idea that we are merely inert parts of a larger causal fabric offends common sense—and is impossible to act upon, since on the determinist scheme, even our thoughts are foreordained. Among other things, we also lose any meaningful sense of morality or of purposive action. Even determinists must act as if they were free causal agents; there is no other way to act.

What the traditional free will-vs.-determinism debate fails to appreciate is that, in general terms, we can—and must—have it both ways. We inhabit a world in which natural and social forces and the human will coexist (however imponderable the relationship). Hitler was a product of German revanchism and of his parents; but Hitler also made decisions that we can only usefully call his own. These twin causal schemes, based respectively in nature and human consciousness, compete, but they need not exclude or deny one another; as a practical matter, they are both indispensable. (Social forces of human origin but beyond the control of most individuals, such as the actions of leaders, or general social or historical conditions, might arguably comprise a separate category.) We comprehend the universe as embracing both natural causal forces (a tree falling, a cell dividing, a comet streaking across the ether) and acts of individual and collective will—everything from opening a door to an act of military conquest.

Thus, the real problem is not which causal framework is better, but how they interrelate. While "soft determinism" may broker the general issue of causality, by recognizing that both free will and external causal forces influence human destiny, how those separate causal spheres mesh, and how to distinguish them, remains a profound human dilemma. And that eternal dilemma—with its implications for our freedom and moral responsibility—creates a foundational spectrum of conflict between simpler and more complex views. It is perhaps the most basic of all moral and political questions.

Whether in emphasizing rehabilitation as well as punishment, or prevention as well as remediation, or considering the unintended effects of aerial eradication of the Colombian coca crop on public health and welfare, what distinguishes the complex perspective is its focus on a wider web of causation: on root sources, secondary and multiplier effects, cycles, dialectical patterns, and distant ramifications. Such causes and effects, as we have noted, are inherently difficult for television to represent, both technically and commercially. Television is a causally challenged medium; it is more episodic than thematic,[42] a medium par excellence of the spot, the moment, the scene. Before-and-after situational comparisons are possible (as they are with still photography); but television naturally focuses on *elapsing* real time, not *elapsed* time or evolutionary progressions. TV news budgets pay for hair styling and traffic helicopters, not for social theorists to explore the complexity of human events.

9 · *Contestability and the Uses of Agnosticism*

We have touched on a range of conceptual polarities that frame the ideological spectrum. Each of these polarities reflects a broader watershed between competing ideological visions; that is, each represents an aspect of the core spectrum between simplicity and complexity. These axes of differentiation may be summarized as follows:

	SIMPLICITY	COMPLEXITY
Ideological Framework:	conservatism	liberalism
Theoretical Frameworks:	positivism	abstraction
	appearance	essence
	literal interpretation; biblical/constitutional fundamentalism	broader and deeper interpretation; "ecological thinking"
Analytic Styles:	formal	synthetic
	logical realism	logical instrumentalism
	partition & distinction	integration & connection
Causal Framework:	existentialism	soft determinism
Social/Political/ Policy Frameworks:	exclusion	inclusion
	inequality	relative economic equality
	laissez-faire	market delimitation and regulation
	simple/passive government	complex/active government
	independence	interdependence
	competition/ confrontation	cooperation
	correction/ retribution	prevention/ intervention

On each of these axes, what distinguishes the left from the right is its relative complexity. In each dimension, that is, the liberal vision conceives a larger moral universe, with a denser network of rights and duties, and one that is more demanding of both individuals and the state. It is a vision that looks beyond the immediately visible to see deeper patterns and systems, contexts and connections, relationships and root causes: a perspective to which electronic media are naturally resistant, and television most of all.

Again, this is not to suggest that the arguments of the left are necessarily more sophisticated or complex than those of the right. It is the underlying values, and corresponding social policies, that are more inclusive, integrated, and complex, however polemical the form of their political expression.[43] While it is no accident that universities remain institutional bastions of American liberalism, not all intellectuals are political complexitarians; one can make sophisticated arguments for the simpler vision, while opposing the axiological complexity of the left. It is equally clear that not all those on the left are complex thinkers; people may be tacit complexitarians for other reasons (even when making simplistic arguments), including self-interest as minority shareholders in the American Dream.

The defining feature, and great polemical asset, of the conservative vision is its relative simplicity. That vision embraces a narrower social contract, and a more polarized spectrum of risk and rewards; fewer constraints on individual conduct, and fewer buffers against other individuals, institutions, or the forces of fate and circumstance; a vision of a Hobbesian world of existential agents (signalled by the emphasis on personal responsibility) with fewer rights and fewer duties. It is an essentially positivist vision: a philosophy of the concrete, the visible, and the obvious.

It is more dissociative than connective and hostile to collectivities and abstract forces: viz. Margaret Thatcher's assertion that
society doesn't exist, only individuals. Such simplicity is precisely what makes conservative messages more telegenic. Wedded to visible scenes, objects, and individuals, television is the
ultimate form of electronic positivism.

In an insightful essay on the American media in the 1980s[44]—
which seems almost to portend the Clinton impeachment—Adam
Gopnik observes that, while both the left and the right profited, in
different ways, from the media's new ethic of aggression,

> . . . in that struggle the far right had a surprising, crucial advantage.
> Left-wing thought in America tends to be extremely abstract—that's
> what makes it so appealing to undergraduates. It offers big, sys-
> tematic explanations of small things. The left has become so deeply
> committed to the notion that consciousness produces reality—
> that cultural politics are the only real politics—that many of its
> members have become content with victories in the field of con-
> sciousness and bored with actual political work. The energy on the
> American left is in cultural studies, not health-care activism. On
> the other hand, right-wing thought in America, even serious right-
> wing thought, tends to be extremely personal. The right, to its
> credit, still believes in the consequences of individual actions, and
> this makes it much better at emphasizing the villainies of individ-
> uals. The right is much better at character assassination, because
> the right still believes in character.

Either of these visions may dominate in the decades to come, but
neither is likely to fade or collapse. Capitalism's productive but
unstable, cyclical, and stratifying character, and democracy's
openness to political debate, jointly ensure the survival of the

ideological spectrum more or less as we know it; and the deeper moral and intellectual foundations of that spectrum lie in our different levels of tolerance of complexity. In a more egalitarian society, there might be less grounds for ideological contention based on immediate self-interest. But even then, it would be theoretically possible for some members (say, those with superior talents) to advocate a return to a less egalitarian society in which the more talented might flourish at the expense of others.

Moreover, each of these broadly polar visions is coherent and respectable. Neither can trump the other with objective or logical proof of its moral or intellectual superiority. No position on the complexity spectrum is objectively better than another; indeed, the notion of objectivity itself can be understood in more or less complex ways. We can agree that murder, assault, rape, theft, fraud, and slavery are unacceptable breaches of moral order. But we inexorably disagree on thresholds of moral harm and responsibility, particularly where the violation is less obvious: where, for instance, on the spectrum of economic relationships between partnership and slavery, exploitation begins; where a specific entity such as a corporation affects the moral interests of a less specific one, such as a geographic or other community; and so forth.

If such disagreements about complexity are, as I believe, paradigmatic instances of what philosophers call "essentially contestable" questions,[45] then we must confront a certain moral and political agnosticism. We cannot ask whether either vision, or some intermediate position, is more plausible or correct from a neutral or objective standpoint; there is no such neutral ground. At this level, we cannot impugn one another's ultimate choices among competing frameworks; it is not even clear to what extent we "choose" them. Perhaps no level or realm of thought more clearly demonstrates this competition between simpler and more complex schemes, and the need for both ideological commitment and a margin of agnosticism, than the intractable dichotomy between free will and determinism: what Auden called "the battle cries of two ideas." The choice between complexity and simplicity is ultimately a subjective preferential one—and a timeless one—about how we organize our world views and value systems.

Where does that leave us, and how do we reconcile such agnosticism with our deeply felt passions and firm convictions? A margin of agnosticism doesn't threaten or undercut our political commitments. But the recognition that those commitments, within dignified limits, have no special claim to superiority should temper them with tolerance, a keener awareness of common and contested ground—and the dignity of ideological argument as such. Like the relative complexity of liberal ideas, the simplicity of conservative ones will always limit their appeal but can never wholly defeat them. So long as it is possible to argue about individual responsibility, acceptable levels of tolerance, the division of wealth, or the relative merits of simpler and more complex frameworks and policies, there is room for both visions, and for a spectrum of robust democratic debate. And so long as television's essential language remains intact, even if its outward technological form is revolutionized, it will unwittingly advance one of those visions and impede the other.

Critical Vision:
Television and the Attentive Society

As individuals and as a nation, we now suffer from social narcissism. The beloved Echo of our ancestors, the virgin America, has been abandoned. We have fallen in love with our own image, with images of our making, which turn out to be images of ourselves.
—Daniel J. Boorstin, *The Image* (1961)

1 · *The Critical Imperative*

Television, to summarize previous chapters, is a relentlessly simplifying and atomizing medium. It simplifies by personalizing and dichotomizing; by truncating and foreshortening events and personalities; by ignoring organic relationships and suppressing uncertainty and ambiguity. It resists contextual and causal complexity and exaggerates the power of individuals as causal agents at the expense of collectivities and social forces. The language of television inflates the importance of certain subjects while ignoring others that are complicated and telephobic. It emphasizes style over substance, appearance over reality, immediacy over remoteness, and physical and emotional conflict over moral, intellectual, or other controversies.

Television is thus biased toward conservatism structurally, as well as for economic and cultural reasons: it is a hospitable platform for the values and messages of the right and hostile to progressive ones. This structural bias is not one of design, but an accident of the medium's nature and language: in sum, its aversion to complexity. What remains to be considered is how such simplicity is manifested in televised discourse, how it militates against progressive ideals, and what remedies, if any, exist for the left.

The simplicity bias is pervasive, encompassing, to a greater or lesser extent, all genres of programming: commercial and public, entertainment and news, commercial advertising and paid political messages. It is especially blatant in the latter format, typified by the notorious thirty-second spot. Among the most creative and deliberately persuasive of messages, these political hand grenades bear the classic hallmarks of propaganda: crude emotional appeals, imagery and symbolism, selectivity and distortion of facts, neglect of inferences and distinctions. They are designed to manipulate emotions and depress reasoning. The antithesis of, and antidote to, such propaganda is the form of discourse known as critical thinking.

Critical thinking is not something abstract or esoteric; a baseline of critical reasoning is vital to the civility and effectiveness of all democratic debate. It begins with adherence to the rules of formal logic, but extends into the realm of "informal logic" to promote clarity, consistency, and completeness, and to expose fallacy, simplification, superficiality, and otherwise weak, irrelevant, or unacceptable arguments.[1] It seeks to disclose the various conceptual and evaluative traps that lurk in simple or blanket statements: false or rigidly binary frameworks; bald claims; concealed interests or motives; neglect of context; disregard for relevant causes or effects, or for key connections or distinctions. Above all, critical thinking *asks questions* that uncritical or polemical discourse aims to ignore or suppress.

On a deeper level, several related principles or tendencies form the intellectual foundations of critical thinking. First, it neither glorifies nor neglects abstractions as tools of the mind. Second, it aims to question or transcend, but not to ignore or deny, what is immediately given or apparent, or what is uncritically asserted or assumed. Third, critical thinkers hold that appearance and reality are neither identical nor unrelated. Fourth, they consider not only visible or obvious causes and effects, but also those which are hidden, remote, multiple, evolutionary, etc. And fifth, whereas propagandists use words purely for effect, critical thinkers distinguish between words or ideas—as maps or representations—and the real terrain that they represent.

Unlike formal logic, critical thinking does not represent a finite set of precise rules, but rather identifies a gray zone of analytical rigor between formal logic and everyday common sense. It relates most of all to several general areas of interface between thought and experience: distinctions and connections; dualities and spectrums; argumentational fallacies; and confusion or obscurity with respect to the character of normative arguments, for instance, the relevance of extrinsic information such as the arguer's commitments or beliefs.[2] Such critical lapses, which might seem obvious enough on the printed page (or might never even appear in print) often go unchecked in the electronic media. TV, the Internet, and talk radio are natural host cultures for such uncritical discourse: excessive, unreasoning partisanship, snap judgements, flat declarations, foolish predictions, unverified rumors, invective, insult, and bluster.

In short, the questions that critical thinkers ask about accuracy, completeness, and rigor are antithetical to the structural and commercial biases of television. Their framework argues for complexity and challenges the simpler, more rigid framework of polemical conservatism.

2 · *The Politics of Simplicity*

The foundational principle of liberalism is the relative complexity of its intellectual and moral-political universe. The liberal project is more ambitious (and the radical one even more so): to redistribute wealth and correct social injustice; to actively promote, and not just to passively allow, opportunities; to protect minorities, preserve nature, regulate the economy, and assert the role of government instrumental to these ends. Conversely, the quintessential feature and great polemical asset of conservatism is its relative simplicity. Smaller government, fewer restrictions on private power, whether corporate or individual, an unregulated market economy—these are the watchwords of the right. There is more freedom from government, but less protection from the predations of other individuals, institutions, or the blind forces of circumstance. Such simplicity may be considered either a virtue or a failing (and arguably in different senses it is both). But either way, it is precisely what makes conservative rhetoric more telegenic.

Moving further to the right, these simpler conservative ideals become crude precepts, which mask a host of uncritical assumptions and myths. Here are a few examples:

○ Democratic government is primarily a threat to individual freedoms, and not their guarantor. Government activism (except for military and police functions) amounts to "throwing money at problems" which can be solved otherwise or left alone.

○ Taxation is tantamount to theft, and public spending equivalent to waste.

○ Unfettered economic markets are just, and business enterprise uniformly serves the public interest.

- Market regulation is merely "red tape" created by "unelected bureaucrats" and thwarts the democratic will of the body politic and the public interest.
- Talent invariably triumphs over circumstance (radical existentialism).
- Rights not expressly enumerated in the Constitution "do not exist."[3]
- The rights of criminals or of the accused (a distinction that is often ignored) compete with the rights of victims.
- Military might equates directly with national security.
- Dissent, especially in wartime, is unpatriotic.
- "Special interests" are running the country or control the liberal agenda, but not the conservative agenda.
- Prayer in public schools is a matter of religious freedom.
- Abortion is murder.[4]
- Homosexuality is immoral and threatens the family.
- Handgun ownership increases personal safety and is protected by the Second Amendment.
- Public funding of the arts only benefits elites.
- Liberals are "soft" and conservatives are "tough."

These are some of the fictions that continue to animate the American right in the aftermath of the Cold War. They appeal at once to self-interest and to our thirst for simplicity: the politics of the self is simpler than that of self-and-others. In comparison to the liberal-complexitarian model, it entails less uncertainty or ambiguity, a more existential causal framework, and a less exacting social contract, based on a lower level of moral reciprocity among individuals.

Flowing from these simplifying assumptions is a wide vocabulary of polemical discourse—symbolically loaded slogans, buzz words, mantras, and shibboleths that typically purport to represent unambivalent good or evil: "tax and spend," "law and order," "family values," "right to work," "class warfare," "right to life," "welfare cheats," "states' rights," "bureaucracy." Liberal consistency—but not conservative—is derided as "knee-jerk." Liberal critics are "naysayers"; those who dare to forecast long-term problems are labeled "gloom and doom"; defenders of the environment are "tree-huggers"; enemies of intolerance are "politically correct."

In this vein, Newt Gingrich's 1994 campaign guide (aptly titled *Language: A Key Mechanism of Control*), encouraged Republican candidates to identify their own campaigns with words such as: environment, freedom, flag, family, humane, youthful, courage, moral. The words it suggested for labeling Democrats included: liberal, betray, corrupt, wasteful, sick, lie, self-serving, and special interest.[5] The latter term has traditionally denoted private economic interests that relied on dollars rather than public support to influence the political process. But in the dominant rhetoric of the right, it has instead come to refer pejoratively (and perversely) to any nonprofit organization advocating some public interest.[6] Such condensation symbols are the hard currency of electronic communication, made to order for television sound bites, and for the simpler, more egocentric values and messages of the right. Precision, accuracy, and depth or complexity of meaning require that they be critically unpacked to reveal what they conceal, compress, or obscure.

While the left (and especially the far left) is not incapable of polemic, there are key differences between the polemics of the left and of the right. An obvious one, which partly begs the question, is that the far right, unlike the far left, is a major political force in the present era. But beyond that, polemics of the left (casual charges of racism or sexism, antinuclear slogans, "jobs and justice," etc.), while simplifying, are hobbled by the inherent complexity of their underlying values and ideals. The right labors under no such handicap, because its values and messages are already simple.

Why have no slogans or buzz words emerged calling for investment in education, child care, or health care? For job training, affordable housing, or preserving the environment? For an adequate but not bloated defense budget, or protecting American jobs and working conditions in a global economy? Where are the snappy sound bites for gun control, tolerance of different lifestyles, collective bargaining, legal aid, or separation of church and state? In the bumper-sticker politics of sound bites and shouting heads, the electronic playing field tilts decidedly to the right.

Uncritical discourse was especially rampant during the Gulf War. While many liberals supported the effort, there was a failure to distinguish between supporting American troops and supporting American policy; criticism of those in the media who tried to cover the war aggressively; the assumption that criticism of military policy is unpatriotic; the notion, espoused by President Bush and others, that the (apparent) military success of American troops and high-tech weaponry against a minor power somehow altered the moral legacies of Vietnam; and the unstated assumption that military triumph, in itself, justified military action.

Again, this is not to say that the left has cornered the market of critical discourse. There is no systematic connection between progressive values and logical rigor, or between dignified conservatism and fallacy. Intricate and sound arguments can be .

made for simpler values, and simple or flawed arguments can be made for more complex values. The best conservative arguments are no more or less logical or reasonable than the best liberal or socialist ones; there is no ultimate principle to appeal to in deciding between them. The simple-complex axis describes a continuum of value systems, not every proponent, argument, tactic, or goal. Likewise, not all conservatives excel on television, nor do all liberals fail. But because polemics and sound bites invariably simplify and shortcut critical thinking, they are the natural tools of the Electronic Right; its rhetoric is far more adaptable to the electronic media environment.

Television has indeed, at certain fateful historic moments, served as an important catalyst for progressive causes: the Army-McCarthy hearings; civil rights; opposition to the Vietnam War; the Watergate hearings. Yet these events have been typified by moments of crisis, providing dramatic visual confrontations between left and right that symbolized much broader and more complicated political currents. (Television was undoubtedly crucial to the influence of charismatic figures such as John F. Kennedy and Martin Luther King, Jr.). In none of these cases, arguably, did TV actually set change in motion; rather, by depicting the flashpoints it more clearly defined the battle lines and tipped the scales, highlighting extreme consequences of conservative policies.[7] Television can vividly depict such flashpoints as isolated symptoms of a conservative political culture. (In August 1992, it exposed the extreme intolerance of party leaders at the Republican National Convention in Houston.) But it is blinkered to the more complex, integrated vision of society that can only emerge if we turn off the tube and look, listen, and think more critically.[8]

This points to a further strategic quandary for progressives in dealing with television and the Electronic Right. The political arguments of the left, center, or right may be equally clever, reasonable, logical, and (to a receptive audience) compelling. But while critical thinking might seem a neutral intellectual toolbox, and an indispensable part of the educational agenda in any field of inquiry, it is also essentially subversive. It inevitably leads not just to the dissecting of arguments but also to the questioning of rhetorical simplicity, authority, hierarchy, vested interests, and the status quo. It promotes precisely the kinds of skepticism and logical and analytic agility that television naturally resists. Thus, it is improbable that conservatives—at least vulgar conservatives—would be anything but implacably opposed to more critical discourse. Such discourse is inimical to the structure and vested commercial interests of television, and to the interests of the Electronic Right.

3 · Critical Viewing and Media Literacy

In a sound bite society, we cannot be critical thinkers without also being critical viewers; the application of critical skills to mass media is therefore an essential counterpart of critical thinking. Media literacy has been defined as "the ability to access, analyze, evaluate, and create messages in various media."[9] Neil Postman uses the term "media ecology" to describe "how the media control the form, distribution, and direction of information, and how such control affects people's cognitive habits, political beliefs, and social relations."[10] Like verbal literacy and critical thinking, it has several important aims: to teach young viewers how to distinguish reality from fantasy and artifice; to examine the distinct codes and cues of visual images, words, music, etc.; to distinguish and decipher commercial, political, and other types of messages; to detect the cynical and the trivial; and in general, to understand how television and other media frame and package information and entertainment, and their influence on viewers, consumers, and citizens.[11]

Students who spend more time watching television than in classrooms, and who have viewed an average of 18,000 TV murders by the time they graduate from high school, must learn to resist television's power to isolate, manipulate, deceive, simplify, palliate, and disguise. They must learn to detect submerged meanings, assess motives, and deconstruct narratives—the very skills we teach them to apply to literature and writing in general. As the boundary between factual messages and advertising is increasingly blurred by "infomercials," "advertorials," and commercialized news, and as corporate advertising creeps insidiously into the school environment, students need to know how to evaluate commercial and political advertising, how news is shaped for a mass audience, and how truth, accuracy, balance, and context are compromised by other interests and imperatives. Moreover, just as literacy involves writing as well as reading, media literacy should include experience in producing and critiquing audiovisual messages. All curriculum development should promote critical thinking; media literacy in particular should be mandatory in the American school curriculum, as it is in Great Britain, Canada, Australia, and elsewhere.

Media literacy cannot focus on television to the exclusion of film, video, radio, music, or the Internet. It must encompass study of the exploding media universe, and its increasingly tenuous relationship to genuine knowledge. (Instead of allocating scarce educational dollars to hardwire American classrooms to the Internet, on the simple assumption that knowledge equates with access to facts, we might better devote those resources to raising the pay and competency standards of teachers.) Nor does critical viewing imply that TV is an evil or all-powerful medium, that it does not gratify legitimate needs and desires, or that children do not bring to it critical faculties of their own. Media literacy should explore TV's positive as well as its negative potentials and the controversies surrounding them. The purpose of critical viewing is not to shield people from television, but to enable them to use and enjoy it intelligently, while recognizing the legitimacy of its sedative and entertaining functions.[12]

Yet, like critical thinking generally, media literacy has an unavoidable ideological dimension. Critical viewing is subversive because, like critical thinking generally, it imparts mental skills which dispositionally favor a more complex view, not just of how television frames and filters reality, but of television itself as a social organism, and of society as a whole. It is subversive because it transfers some of the power over the message and its interpretation from the mediators (typically commercial enterprises) to the audience—democratic citizens. It is inherently skeptical, egalitarian, and anticommercial. It posits motives, causes, and contextual factors that interested parties would prefer to ignore. Thus, media literacy is bound to offend conservatives who would deny its relevance to informed citizenship. Like the Wizard of Oz, media corporations and advertisers will inevitably oppose (or in more sinister cases, co-opt and corrupt) efforts to look behind the curtain and reveal how they manipulate.

But there is also an important, if limited, political counterclaim to be made here. Media literacy is not simply "proliberal" or "anticonservative." In principle, it should appeal to dignified conservatives who value individual opportunity and citizenship over corporate hegemony. Open societies must tolerate many moral complexities and ostensible contradictions, including some things that warrant critical scrutiny, or even condemnation, but not wholesale proscription. On paramount issues such as the value of informed democratic citizenship, which at least partly transcend ideology, thoughtful conservatives will side with liberals. In this sense, the critical thinking and viewing agenda is not just a liberal one but a broader democratic one.[13]

4 · Critical Dialogue and Democratic Citizenship

Certain progressive goals in the twenty-first century relate to more nebulous aspects of the American political-media culture. For example, that culture would survive if it tolerated more open discussion of class. Progressives have a particular stake in ending this taboo because their views on the subject of class are at greater variance with the status quo. Class mobility exists in America, up to a point, as does stratification, with intertwining racial, ethnic, educational, and economic barriers. The existence of such barriers in a market-driven society—and the acceptable range, and the costs of eliminating or reducing them—are not just valid but crucial matters of debate. In a more mobile and egalitarian society there would be less to differ about; then, we could all become conservatives. As it is, we dream two American Dreams: in the rosier conservative one, we are a society without obvious or eradicable barriers to class mobility; in the liberal one, it is not so simple.

More broadly, a culture of critical thinking and viewing would demand higher standards for media, government, and citizens alike. For instance, it would demand greater journalistic accountability both ethically and intellectually, on matters such as integrity and fairness, concealed bias, diligence, accuracy, and news judgement. News producers and consumers alike should understand how television drives, alters, and distorts events—and how covering them differently, or not at all, might serve or disserve a wider public interest. This cannot be done by the media alone, or on a judicial model of self-appointed news councils. An excellent place to begin, with strong public support, would be to make a clear distinction between the private and public lives of public figures. It isn't so difficult. Journalists can learn to just say no.

A more media-literate nation would not tolerate news media that accept evasive answers from politicians or shrink from offending them with a follow-up question, or buckle under corporate threats of litigation should inconvenient facts be exposed to consumers. It would not brook the barring of reporters from a battlefield where Americans are fighting, or countenance contempt for the press on the part of public officials, which is properly regarded as contempt for the people. When a president plays on public mistrust of the media by treating reporters like a pack of baying dogs, or deflecting their questions amid the whir of a waiting helicopter, we should have the critical sense to be affronted at this insult to democracy.

A media-literate audience would be more critical, not less, of individual news media—but not reflexively critical. Instead of carping about media negativism, it would insist on getting the bad news as well as the good: "My country right or wrong," said Carl Schurz, "when right to be kept right; when wrong to be put right."

As it is, Americans' mistrust of the media, as of politicians, is often uncritical: not based on performance, or on democratic criteria, but questioning the very legitimacy of those institutions. This is not just a failure to recognize the abundant examples of journalistic excellence, but indifference to the functions of news media in a democracy. Such broad based delegitimation of the media (and of Congress) is not just a vague threat to a democratic culture; it's a deep flaw in the fabric. Like government, the Media R Us; we elect them, from the choices available, every time we buy a periodical or tune into a broadcast. And we elect them for terms of our own choosing, lasting minutes or seconds.

In the human mind, neuroses arise as conflicts within the self that affect our perceptions and relationships. Likewise, in the public mind certain uncritical myths, perpetuated by the media and politicians, function as collective neuroses that distort our perceptions and behavior and the very climate of debate. While typically containing grains of truth that strike deep emotional chords in the national psyche, they also represent failures of critical thinking, and the failure to acknowledge our collective capacity and responsibility for political action or inaction.

Among the salient examples of such neuroses are indiscriminate hostility toward political incumbents and toward the media —institutions which are currently perceived more as alien forces than as imperfect mirrors of society. The anti-incumbent neurosis ignores the fact that we freely re-elect some 98 percent of officeholders, as well as the main reason for high incumbency rates: the system of political finance. Thus, Republican enthusiasm for term limits was cured by the reality therapy of electoral success in 1994.[14]

Public mistrust of the news media reflects a similar pattern. Many news outlets (like many politicians) are shallow, sensational, dishonest, inaccurate, or scurrilous. We should be more critical of the media for specific failures and lapses, such as self-censorship or allowing corporate influence on news decisions; but less critical of the media for performing their function as surrogate messengers and watchdogs. A blind mistrust of either sector is a civic neurosis. Politics is sometimes futile, and politicians and the media are sometimes corrupt; but to hold these beliefs reflexively only reveals the low self-esteem of American democracy. In fact, it matters very much how the news is reported, whom we elect to represent us, and how those representatives conduct our business. It matters because lives, freedoms, and billions of dollars are at stake, including our own.

A more critical attitude here requires that we make a series of elementary, but routinely ignored, distinctions. The most important such distinction is between the paramount value of a free press and the quality of its performance. Thus, in addition to media-literacy curricula, greater democratic accountability demands more public criticism of, and self-criticism by, the press. Broadcasting, in particular, is devoid of such criticism; like print and cyberspace, it needs more independent critics and ombudsmen. At the same time, every democratic citizen should be educated for and capable of some level of informed media criticism. News media are not an afterthought of democratic life.

Another elementary distinction that we routinely obscure, when it suits our rhetorical purposes, is that between fair criticism and censorship. We degrade the First Amendment by impressing it into use as a shield against all criticism. Criticism does not threaten freedom of speech; it is not censorship. We need to distinguish between the rightness of an utterance and the right to say it; between the message and the messenger; and between a proper respect for quality and what philistines call "elitism." The American media have many shortcomings, based on commercialism and on ordinary human imperfection; but a mindless contempt for the media based on fear and ignorance is not the answer to the real and remediable problems of gathering and telling the news. It is rather a kind of bigotry toward informed citizenship.

5 · *The Attentive Society: Journalism and Ideological Literacy*

E.J. Dionne, Jr., has written that, "Lurking beneath the widespread criticism of the media is the sense that something is deeply defective in the public debate itself and that the press is not taking on a role that it ought to embrace: to make that debate more accessible, coherent and honest."[15] For that to happen, media producers and consumers alike must become more ideologically literate. We must begin with agreement about indisputable facts; that is one of journalism's essential functions. But facts are only where we start from. Interesting and important debates are never about facts per se; they are about how we interpret them, and which facts are more relevant to some larger question or principle. Interesting arguments are not about facts, but about values: in effect, about the extent and complexity of our role as our brothers' and sisters' keepers.

Ideology is like weather: we may not like it, but it won't go away. To suggest that it is bad or unnecessary is a form of denial which, like blanket contempt for the media or government, can only impoverish debate. Awash in sound bites and electronic propaganda, both political and commercial, in clashing images, personalities, and parties, young Americans need to understand the ideas and values underlying different points on the spectrum, and the nature of the spectrum itself. Conservatives should embrace their simplicity; progressives should take equal pride in an agenda based on a more demanding and complicated social compact.

Greater ideological literacy is especially needed in the news media, which both lead and follow society at large. This does not mean that journalists should share any particular outlook, or should become philosophers; rather, they need greater understanding of, and respect for, the range of democratic ideological debate. This applies equally, of course, to politicians and their spokesmen, pundits, academicians, and their audiences.[16] In an ideologically literate society, politicians would identify with their visions, not blur them; citizens and journalists would respect both the legitimacy and the proper boundaries of partisanship. They would distinguish between the political strength of arguments and their moral force; between the political status of the left or the right at a given moment, and the validity of their claims or broader goals; between issues amenable to neutral problem solving and those on which there can never be complete political consensus. Such distinctions are frequently obscured in a sound bite society, and most often at the expense of the left.

We should distinguish, further, between fiscal prudence—government not spending more than it takes in—and fiscal priorities: how much, and for what purposes, the government should take in and spend. We should distinguish between government regulation in the public interest and authoritarian government; between our individual notions of the good life, and the collective value of our common freedom to pursue those individual goods. Making such distinctions is a quintessential liberal project, and one that dignified conservatives and radicals can share.

What E.J. Dionne, Jr. and Glenn Tinder have called an "attentive society" is not a grand mutual pursuit of truth; truth is crucial, but only as a premise for the conduct of dignified argument. Neither is it the pursuit of universal consensus on all important issues, which the complexity spectrum precludes.[17] It is rather about a higher level of understanding and respect. As Christopher Lasch has written, "what democracy requires is vigorous public debate, not [just] information."[18] In a society where journalists often wield more influence than public officials, the quality of political representation, public discourse, journalism, and mass education are closely intertwined. Like our schools, television has the potential to contribute to a more, and not less, attentive society. It is erroneous to suppose that what we teach our children, and what television teaches them, about tolerance, democratic conversation, or ideology, are not similarly intertwined. The objective of journalism, writes Dionne,[19] should be

> to salvage [Walter] Lippmann's devotion to accuracy and fairness by putting these virtues to the service of the democratic debate that [John] Dewey so valued. This means, in turn, that journalism needs to be concerned with far more than its professional rules and imperatives.

Whatever their particular failings, the media as a whole constitute the only portion of the private sector that is protected by the Constitution and essential to the democratic process. That is why quality, and not just quantity or profits, is important. Among other things, we have lost sight of the purpose of journalistic competition; the public would be better served if journalists worried less about getting it first, and more about getting it best. Certain elements of the media inevitably will—and should—focus on the impregnation of celebrities by alien visitors. But if the need for bread and circuses cannot be dismissed, neither can the need for quality in the flow of information relevant to democratic life, and for education that builds the demand for it.

American journalism is founded on a glorious contradiction. Virtually all of it is commercially based or market dependent, even in the nonprofit sector. It is sometimes compromised, and always limited, by that dependence and its attendant pressures. In this sense, the media can't help being conservative. Yet while the media must sell, they also have a democratic mission to inform, and to provide a forum for debate; and for these reasons the journalistic enterprise has inherently liberal and democratic tendencies: tendencies which, contrary to their commercial foundations, challenge power, question authority, and empower ordinary citizens by diffusing information more widely than corporate or private interests would like. Thus, however ensconced in the private sector, serious journalism—like public libraries and public education—also has an intrinsically egalitarian public purpose.

There are several important ways in which this dilemma can be mitigated. One is a diverse and competitive environment of media pluralism—which the present media oligopoly is not. Another is for the mainstream media to follow the polestar of being fierce advocates—for democratic argument. The civic journalism movement has got it half right: we need journalism that promotes active and informed citizenship. What we don't need is journalism driven by surveys, opinion polls, or focus groups, which is market research masquerading as democracy.

To service democratic debate, the media must understand and respect all shades of opinion, and the dignity of ideological argument. Television's harsh, impatient gaze—oriented toward means and gamesmanship rather than ends, issues, or values; quick to expose scandal and flaws of character, slow to consider deeper motives or broader intentions or ideas—is part of the problem. In its institutional cynicism it inhibits and ignores serious ideological debate; hence the persistence of the naive supposition that bipartisan "solutions" can be found to important problems, and that partisanship is merely a fog obscuring the real political terrain, and not, in fact, the terrain itself.[20] And when ideology is scanted, complex ideology is taxed disproportionately.[21]

If facts are only a point of departure for democratic discourse, then journalism schools, an awkward anomaly within the American university with no clear public purpose or intellectual focus, ought to provide more than vocational training for the harvesting of facts (or worse, the unseemly commingling of truth and propaganda, in misalliance with advertising and public relations). To suggest that journalists are not merely brokers of information but educators, who should themselves be students of human values and society, is to realize both the vital role of the journalism profession and the deep impatience with real knowledge—about ideas, theories, and values—in American culture.

Instead of just teaching people how to produce journalism—a misuse of our national educational resources—we should teach them to be better critics and consumers of journalism. In effect, we need to relocate journalism education to the elementary and secondary levels, to educate younger Americans about the technical, economic, and moral imperatives of the media. In short, America needs less journalism education, and more media education. While the two are not mutually exclusive, it is far more important for kids to learn what goes into doing and using journalism, than for young adults to learn how to meet a deadline. And instead of just training and credentializing reporters, producers, and Webmasters, universities should prepare them for their wider role as educators.

Information—to return to our introductory theme—is indeed

power. That is no mere sound bite. But there is also a deep and naive faith in American culture: that all information is equally useful, and we can never have too much of it; that a rising information tide lifts all boats; that information is somehow tantamount to wisdom, mastery, or sensitivity. We need more critical thinking and robust debate—not just the classic American quick fix of more technology. The Internet may be bountiful, but so is the local public library or the inspiring teacher. The Web won't save us, or make our children smarter, and neither will the simplistic policy of putting more computers in classrooms.

Real education—whether the medium be TV, video, computer, radio, a classroom, or a park bench—admits no such technological shortcuts. It is not about the glutting of minds with facts, but the culture of critical thinking and respectful debate. It is not, said Yeats, the filling of a pail, but the lighting of a fire. Commercial television, more than anything else in our society, undercuts those values by inuring us, and our political and media surrogates, to solutions that are easy, visible, quick, cheap, short-term, and simple.

As Roderick Hart and others have urged, a new critical ethic of the moving image is needed for the twenty-first century. More than that, the sheer scope and complexity of the fusion between politics and the media warrant a new avenue of scholarly inquiry, combining the tools and techniques of media studies, moral and political discourse, and the social and information sciences, to explore the cognitive, psychological, political, and behavioral impact of all visual and interactive media, especially on children.

One option for the left, in the face of the corporate media oligopoly, lies in alternative sources of media production and distribution, in areas such as public access TV, microradio, and the

Internet. The good news is that the cost of media production is declining; and here video, cable, and the Internet offer real possibilities. But so long as commercial television retains its dominance, and public television remains underfunded and subservient to political and private interests, market economics remains a powerful barrier to alternative voices. Ultimately, quality journalism, alternative or otherwise, will remain a ghetto until some information media are decommercialized, and until America invests more heavily in its schools.

Even with additional resources and channels, the structural barriers remain. These barriers at least partly explain why alternative programming efforts, in Graham Knight's words, "often turn out to be, in comparison with mainstream television, dull, long-winded, and sanctimonious. . . ."[22] What is important, Knight concludes, "is not [the appropriation of existing] techniques per se (*as if they had some naturalized ideological essence*), [my italics] but rather how they are combined and used." This book has argued that there is precisely such a 'naturalized ideological essence' in the media, against the grain of which progressives must labor.[23]

6 · Roadblocks and Remedies

Two orthodoxies have historically served as the great sea anchors of American culture, blunting and deferring its collisions with modernity. One is religious fundamentalism; the other is market fundamentalism, the simple, uncritical gospel of unlimited enterprise, growth, and consumption. They are forces of tradition and moral certainty, each rooted in radical simplicity: the authoritarian simplicity of scriptural authority, on one hand, and the anarchic simplicity of market authority on the other. A third

American orthodoxy, more subtly reactionary in its implications, and linked to faith in the market, is scientism, a blind faith in technology.

Each of these dogmas exempts us from thinking about moral and political complexities, and the responsibilities of thought and action. But as simplifying codes for personal and public conduct, and walls around our insecurities of status and meaning—dividing us by class, race, and conscience—they are also forces of inequality and intolerance. Television, without intent or design, has failed to challenge, and in important ways has advanced each of these orthodoxies, while impeding the countervailing forces of diversity, equality, inclusion, and renewal: in sum, of a more complex society.

How might these orthodoxies be opposed by the left? Most political problems admit of some form of political remedy, whether legislative change or electoral challenge, policy or institutional reform, or consciousness raising through public protest or the media themselves. There is no such silver bullet available to the left in confronting the Electronic Right. As was suggested earlier, even the relatively innocuous goal of increasing media literacy is not free of political pitfalls. Television's systematic hostility to progressive values and messages represents a basic structural and institutional problem for liberalism, and not just a problem of reforming the content of TV programming, its accessibility to liberal voices, or even the structure of ownership of electronic media. I have not suggested that television can be retooled as an agent of progressive values, but have merely tried to identify some of the impediments it poses to the complex ideal of a more democratic nation, with a more expansive and inclusive middle class. However, there are many ways in which television might do a better job, not just for liberals or conservatives, but for democracy.

Some of the suggestions that follow have been made elsewhere and bear repeating. They are signposts toward the more distant and fundamental reforms—centered around public (nonprofit), rather than state or private, control of public life—that will be necessary to democratize the American media and society in the new century. We need to find alternatives both to state bureaucracies and corporate McNews, as well as to the power of corporate religion and foundations dependent upon corporate largesse. Other democracies, some of which owe their existence or survival to American blood and treasure, enjoy such alternatives, and in consequence, higher standards of civic discourse.[24] We deserve the same.

Driven by technology, contemporary life is clearly becoming more complex, bringing greater range and intricacy to human relationships: for example, through advances in medicine, the advent of cyberspace, and worldwide economic integration. These changes in turn make it harder for democratic societies to define and police the moral boundaries between individual agents—or even, as the debates about abortion and euthanasia suggest, to determine who is a moral agent. But it is also clear that social complexity does not automatically engender greater complexity of vision. If anything, the opposite is true: daunted by their exposure to television's "Mean World," and the bewildering changes around them, people seek political refuge in simple, self-regarding values and dissociation from others.

Above all else, the revival of a robust American left will require recognition of the existence and scope of its television problem, and of the related telecommunications issues that affect the very terms and parameters of political debate. The liberal revival will also require specific, aggressive countermeasures: education and social and media criticism that expose the polemical distortion, simplification, and fallacies of the Electronic Right.

None of the connections between television and conservatism outlined in this book is more important than the brute fact that both are contemptuous of American children. We need as a nation to take our children more seriously; they are both overexposed and uniquely vulnerable to TV messages. Broadcasters have brazenly defied pressure from the FCC, the public, and the mandate of the Children's Television Act of 1990, to provide more and better educational programming for children. Both in quality and quantity, what now passes for children's programming to meet FCC guidelines is a national disgrace. "Over and over again," says Peggy Charren, a leading advocate for children's television, "America's TV industry has demonstrated that, absent close regulation, it doesn't give a damn about service to children."[25] Among other conditions for licensure, there should be a weekly minimum of independently produced children's programming on commercial stations. We must teach children to watch TV with discrimination, but we also need better programming for children on the public airwaves (or digital spectrum). And we need to understand how juvenile viewing affects cognitive and emotional skill development, both for better and for worse.

Free speech in the political marketplace—not paid speech determined by the economic marketplace—is the jewel in the crown of American democracy. It is a right envisioned by the Framers as accruing to individuals, not to corporate entities. But with television as the most powerful soapbox, our public life has been suffocated by private wealth and commercial forces. It is time to decouple profits and power: to separate wealth and commerce from political discourse. This emphatically does not mean regulating speech content or further diluting the First Amendment. On the contrary, it means insulating our democratic conversation from the capricious and unequal influence of money, and the flagrant corruption of access and influence peddling. "The cost of TV time-buys," said then-FCC Chairman Reed Hundt in 1995,[26]

> makes fundraising an enormous entry barrier for candidates for public office, an oppressive burden for incumbents who seek re-election, a continuous threat to the integrity of our political institutions, and a principal cause of the erosion of public respect for public service.

Since 1896, when the Supreme Court established the doctrine of "separate but equal" in *Plessy v. Furgeson,* no ruling has so thoroughly compromised the democratic ideal of political equality in the interests of race, religion, or class. But arguably the worst decision of the twentieth century was *Buckley v. Valeo* (1976), which established campaign spending as a form of freedom of speech. Any agenda to advance American democracy must include the reversal of that decision. Many other democracies have banned all paid political advertising, at no cost to the vitality of their democratic debate. Even banning political ads, which provided $400 million in broadcasting revenues in 1996, would deprive broadcasters of less than two percent of their total advertising revenues, estimated to be about $30 billion.

In addition to media literacy, and removing the political-cash nexus through genuine campaign finance reform, the left must redefine and reassert the broader public interest in the area of telecommunications as the digital age dawns. The specific goals here are not a mystery. They are long-range and ambitious, but vital to a democratic media environment.[27] They include:

o Reversal by the Supreme Court of *Buckley v. Valeo*.

o Repeal of the Telecommunications Act of 1996. This enormous piece of corporate mischief, putatively designed to foster diversity and competition, and passed with little congressional debate or public airing, has had precisely the opposite effect—relaxing ownership rules and leading to another round of megamergers and acquisitions. The only obstacle to repeal is a Congress indentured to the status quo and deep in the pocket of media interests. Our government has dispensed the public air- and radio waves to private interests with uncommon generosity; but all good things come to an end. Competition and healthy profits have a place in the information sector of a democratic society; oligopoly and obscene profits do not.

o Public hearings on the passage of antitrust legislation—and enforcement of existing statutes—to reimpose limits on ownership of broadcast licenses by single companies and in single markets, including strict separation of information content and transmission conduits.[28]

o Cable TV has provided better, more diverse, and more civically relevant programming for affluent subscribers. But a democratic media system will require cable access for all citizens and institutions.

o In place of the failed and commercialized public television system, America needs a new public media system for the twenty-first century: a venue for diversity, excellence, and public access, as was envisioned in the Carnegie Commission report that led to the establishment of public broadcasting in 1967. The funding mechanism must guarantee the system's independence from government, corporations, and foundations. As Robert W. McChesney argues, charging broadcasters a fee for use of the digital spectrum could generate $2 billion to $5 billion that would subsidize "an extraordinary nonprofit and noncommercial broadcasting system"; the federal expenditure for public broadcasting is now a paltry quarter of a billion.[29] Meanwhile, the FCC under Reed Hundt (1993-1997) raised more than $20 billion through auctions of parts of the radio spectrum, but was unable to prevent Congress's giveaway of space (estimates of its worth range beyond $70 billion) on the expanded spectrum that digital television has made possible.

Lawrence K. Grossman, among others, has proposed an annual spectrum fee to be paid into a public trust fund for a noncommercial "multimedia educational and information electronic freeway," including public and community access stations.[30] Such a system could also be funded through taxes on commercial media and on advertising; and through the auctioning of the analog spectrum, once the transition to digital is effected. Royalties on the use of airwaves to fund public TV were first proposed by Walter Lippmann in the 1930s. Private broadcasters reap enormous profits from using the public airwaves and digital spectrum at no cost—a palpable absurdity—and cable operators pay only nominal amounts for their local monopolies.

Among other things, this freeway should provide airtime to political parties and candidates. Virtually every other developed country makes airtime available to candidates and prohibits the purchase of time; if Brazil can do this, so can we. Free time for parties and candidates goes hand-in-hand with public financing of federal elections. If our electoral system isn't worth making fully democratic, nothing is. The canard that limits or bans on political spending abridge free speech, or would involve government "control" of political speech, must be challenged. We must learn to distinguish between democratic public regulation—government of, by, and for the people—and authoritarian control.

The freeway should also provide commercial-free, quality educational and entertainment programming for American children, as well as for schools, libraries, hospitals, prisons, and other institutions. It should treat its audience "as participating citizens instead of mere consumers."[31] There is a clear precedent for such public interest use of the electronic frontier in the Morrill Land Grant Act (1862), which gave federal land to the states to finance colleges.

- The United States should follow the Swedish example and ban all commercials and "product-related programming" aimed at children.[32]
- Another long overdue project that could be funded by spectrum fees and taxes on advertising would be an independent national research center on electronic media.

Remedies are clearly available for the problems of political finance and corporate control of the media. What is lacking is the political will to assert that the American people, not stockholders, own the airwaves and digital spectrum. Until that happens, can we count on the rapidly commercializing Internet to end the stranglehold of a few corporate giants on American culture? Alternatively, if the present system makes sense, why not also turn over our national parks for commercial development and

reap the revenues from higher admission fees, concessions, bill-
board advertising, and marketing tie-ins and spin-offs?

7 · *The Critical Spirit*

At least until television itself, in whatever evolving form, becomes
a battleground of criticism and debate, it will remain an essentially conservative technology: isolating, narcotizing, trivializ-
ing, commercializing, reflecting a simpler moral universe. The
left must challenge that model of electronic citizenship. It must
envision a future in which television is more independent and
informative and serves a more attentive public: a nation not of
intellectuals or cultural elitists but of critical thinkers and viewers, for whom TV is more than a plug-in drug.

It is not so wild a dream. The right will resist the propagation
of critical attitudes and media and political literacy. It will exploit
and defend the status quo of deregulated commercial television,
which has been crucial to its recent success. But the elite that the
right fears the most is not the cultural one of liberal professionals and intellectuals. It is rather the far more dangerous one that
liberalism aims to create: a sophisticated and critical information
elite consisting of every American citizen.

Uncommon visionaries can view their times as if from outside,
and even glimpse the future; I make no such claim. But the evidence strongly suggests that we are living in a brittle, decaying
era that will soon seem like a distant memory. It is obvious to most
of us that American democracy is awry, its citizens distrustful, cynical, and alienated from the interlocking power centers that form
the corporate-political-media complex. The coming shocks could
bring about democratic renewal, or further polarization and crisis along the fault lines of the great orthodoxies: between the

haves and have-nots, the tolerant and the intolerant, the plugged-in and the unplugged.

The rush of technology will influence these upheavals, but in no way assures their harmonious resolution: only new possibilities, and new areas of contention. We have clung too long to a naive faith in the moral potentials of the machine. Television, computers, automobiles—these tools have altered and enriched our private existence; but far from enriching our public life and bringing us together, they have mainly kept us apart. Expecting deliverance through technology is like asking a washing machine to clean our conscience, or a television set to watch our children. As American democracy is tested on anvils unknown, the only genuine progress will be post-technological, and toward greater democracy.

Liberalism falters on television and radio most of all because, unlike the polemical pyrotechnics of the right, it is serious and complex. It is not about forms of separation and domination—such as buccaneering capitalism, or narrow and insular social values—but about real "family values": health, education, jobs, children, a clean environment, worker safety, and fairness—in sum, the American Dream of upward mobility and an ever-expanding middle class. It's boring on radio because it isn't bigoted and doesn't test the limits of free speech. It's boring on TV because it's intricate and egalitarian and challenges passivity and narcissistic emotions. But it isn't irrelevant and it won't go away. Progressive values, however mocked or ignored by the media, express lasting, important human needs.

While the various egalitarian principles differentiate left from right, liberalism does not simply reduce to those identifiable precepts. It is also a different way of seeing the world, marked by intellectual tolerance and flexibility, an appetite for complexity, and a critical spirit. That spirit, in turn, cannot be exhaustively catalogued, but it includes attention to causes and context; to ambiguities, contradictions, and vested interests; to latent or underlying connections and distinctions; to the priority of reality over appearance, and of public over commercial values. It is inimical to a medium that is wedded to the here and now, the flat assertion, the symbolic word or image, and the credulous acceptance of the visible.

The critical spirit is analytical and skeptical, questioning images and arguments, probing and reassessing the competing claims and divergent realities of different individuals and groups. It is the elixir that kept Norberto Bobbio afloat in a darker time than our own, amid the fierce ideological crosscurrents of the Italian left in the early years of the Cold War:[33]

> . . . the most salutary fruits of the European intellectual tradition, the value of enquiry, the ferment of doubt, a willingness to dialogue, a spirit of criticism, moderation of judgement, philological scruple, a sense of the complexity of things.

Notes

Introduction

1. See, for example, J.S. Nye, Jr., & W.A. Owens, "America's Information Edge," *Foreign Affairs* 75:2 (March/April 1996): 20–36.

2. As Philip Kipper points out, HDTV by itself "doesn't make the medium any smarter . . . [it] won't create any remarkable change in the way viewers use television, nor will it significantly alter the kind of information they can extract from it." (P. Kipper, "The Computer Television Marriage," *Television Quarterly* XXV:3 (1991): 13.) HDTV is not even, strictly speaking, a breakthrough technology; it was the result of a decade of tedious work in the 1980s on improving computer codes to make existing digital technology more efficient, especially in compressing data for transmission in order to achieve finer resolution onscreen. Nor was this research simply a case of bold free enterprise; it was done largely at the instigation of the Federal Communications Commission to counter the threat of Japanese domination of the HDTV market.

3. "The Magic Box," *The New Yorker*, April 11, 1994: p. 45.

4. I especially recommend the works of Neil Postman, Jerry Mander, Marie Winn, and Roderick Hart.

5. The notion of liberalism's obsolescence is part of the flotsam of the recent conservative tide, even as the deficits rung up by the Reagan and Bush administrations, more than tripling the national debt, have served to justify government retrenchment. To put to rest the end-of-your-ideology thesis, see Norberto Bobbio's excellent short work *Left and Right: The Significance of a Political Distinction* (Chicago: University of Chicago Press, 1996).

6. Michael Lind, for example, proposes such a four-fold matrix in *Up from Conservatism: Why the Right is Wrong for America* (New York: The Free Press, 1996). As Lind observes, there is a populist aspect to the social conservatism of the religious right: a fear of large institutions of government and business alike; but that populism doesn't make it egalitarian. Lind also notes a new threat to the individual's sense of economic security in America and other post-industrial societies, in the form of the emerging global economy.

7. An example is Graham Knight's brilliant analysis of tabloid television, "The Reality Effects of Tabloid Television," in M. Raboy and P.A. Bruck, eds., *Communication For and Against Democracy* (Montreal & New York: Black Rose Books, 1989). The genre also includes the works of Theodore Adorno, Douglas Kellner, Murray Edelman, and many others. On the other hand, it is questionable whether there even exists a conservative "theory" of media; media criticism on the right consists mainly of claims that the mainstream media are liberal-biased.

8. Videos and VCRs have partially blurred the boundary between TV and feature film production; and the late 1990s saw increasing creative crossover between the two entertainment universes.

9. G. Gerbner, "Television: The New State Religion?" *Et cetera* 34:2 (June 1977): 148.

10. L. Loevinger, "The Limits of Technology," *Television Quarterly* 6:1 (Winter 1967): 11. It might be argued, however, that while even "bad" TV serves important functions, these include dumbing us all down, and defining what and who are "common," while pretending to offer what we want, rather than what will maximize profit.

11. "How Synthetic Experience Shapes Social Reality," *Journal of Communication* 40:2 (Spring 1990): 85.

12. Numerous studies, for example, suggest that violence on television causes violence in society. There is certainly violence enough in both spheres; and it is not implausible that the flow of causal influence is stronger from TV to society than vice versa. A. Wurtzel wrote in 1977 that, "By far the largest number of studies have established a relationship between violent programming and aggressive behavior, although the results must necessarily be viewed with caution . . . while there is no clear-cut, definitive *proof* that such a relationship exists, the evidence points strongly in that direction." ("Television Violence and Aggressive Behavior," *Et cetera* 34:2 (June 1977): 223).

13. Gerbner, "Television's Populist Brew: The Three B's," *Et cetera* 44:1 (Spring 1987): 6.

14. Contra Gerbner, Michael J. Robinson, and Clifford Zukin found (*Journal of Communication*, Spring 1976) that, even controlling for education, age, occupation, and political party, there was a high correlation between dependency on television as opposed to print media, and support for George C. Wallace in the 1968 election. "In fact," they write, "the relationship between

television dependency and support for Wallace was *stronger* among the more highly educated, the older, and those with higher incomes." The correlation was most pronounced among Democrats and Independents, among whom "there was a marked tendency for television reliance to correspond with the Nixon vote as well as the Wallace vote."

15. See, for example, Jeff Greenfield's "TV is Not the World," *Columbia Journalism Review* (May-June, 1978): 29-34.

16. *ibid.*, p. 31.

Chapter I

1. Bishop [Madison Social Text Group], "The New Right and the Media," *Social Text* 1:1 (Winter 1979): 178.

2. History may judge the 1994 midterm election an anomaly; for whatever reasons, the Republican majority class of 1994, elected on the "Contract for America" in the wake of Clinton's failed health care reform campaign, was far more conservative, and more ideological, than the voters who elected them.

3. The percentage of centrists in the House and Senate, according to a 1996 report by Sarah Binder of the Brookings Institution, has declined since 1969 from approximately one-third to ten percent. Similarly, many traditionally competitive states, including Florida, North Carolina, New York, Wisconsin, Minnesota, and Oregon, have elected Republican senators seemingly well to the right of their electorates; the same can hardly be said for Democrats on the state or national level.

4. See *Extra!* 8:2 (March/April 1995), 14.

5. As reported in the *New York Times* (March 13, 1997, p. B10), the ten largest Republican leadership PACs (distributing money

to various Congressional candidates) in the 1995–1996 election cycle had total receipts of more than $12.9 million. The smallest of the ten had receipts of $433,000. In contrast, only two of the top ten Democratic leadership PACs received over $200,000, and the total receipts of the ten was slightly over $2.6 million — considerably less than the $4.5 million that the largest Republican leadership PAC, GOPAC, raised all by itself.

6. Not all of these claims can be made unequivocally, however. Michael Arlen, for example, argues incisively (in *The View from Highway* 1) that TV journalism contributed to the escalation, as well as to the eventual de-escalation, of the Vietnam War.

7. Although these gatekeepers are not all conservatives, a feedback loop governs their choices of guests, so that, with conservatives in more dominant positions, fewer liberals (and especially left-liberals) are chosen to appear. Compare, for example, the prominence of Jerry Falwell or Pat Robertson with that of the liberal clergy.

8. (unsigned commentary) *The New Yorker*, Oct. 29, 1990.

9. H. Kurtz, *Hot Air: All Talk, All the Time* (New York: Times Books, 1996), p. 335.

10. See, for example, J. Baggaley et al., *Psychology of the Television Image* (New York: Praeger, 1980), and J. Condry, *The Psychology of Television* (Hillsdale, NJ: Lawrence Erlbaum Associates, 1989).

11. A survey of high school and college students has reported "a strong relationship between 'involvement with television' (i.e., heavy exposure together with perceptions that the medium was personally important and influential) and a personality syndrome characterized by acceptance of conventional social values, adher-

ence to prevailing norms, and avoidance of behaviors proscribed by the larger society." (R.H. Wiegel, "American Television and Conventionality," *Journal of Psychology* 94:2 (1976): 253.)

12. J. Mander, *Four Arguments for the Elimination of Television* (New York: Quill, 1978), p. 168.

13. R. Stam, "Television News and Its Spectator" in E.A. Kaplan, ed., *Regarding Television*.

14. Gitlin, *The Twilight of Common Dreams: Why America is Wracked by Culture Wars.* (New York: Metropolitan Books, 1995) p. 64.

15. The American Psychological Association's 1992 report on television notes [p. 22] that "In comparison with their proportions in the population, children, elderly people, minorities, women, and gays and lesbians are all underrepresented in television programming." (A.C. Huston, et al., *Big World, Small Screen: The Role of Television in American Society*, [Lincoln, NE: U. of Nebraska Press, 1992]). Arguably, minorities, homosexuals, and independent women have appeared in significant numbers on TV only in the wake of societal changes that made room for them.

16. TV has created what George Gerbner has called a "nonselectively used cultural pattern which can no longer serve the tasks of cultivating selective and differentiated group, class, or other public consciousness." (G. Gerbner, "Television: The New State Religion?" *Et cetera* 4:2 (June 1977): 149).

17. See, for example, T.J. Volgy, and J.E. Schwarz, "TV Entertainment Programming and Sociopolitical Attitudes," *Journalism Quarterly* 57:1 (Spring 1980): 150–155.

18. J. Fallows, *Breaking the News: How the Media Undermine American Democracy* (New York: Pantheon Books, 1996), 142.

NOTES   199

19. J. Condry, "Thief of Time, Unfaithful Servant: Television and the American Child" *Daedalus* 122:1 (Winter 1993): p. 264.

20. Or as James F. Lea writes in *Political Consciousness and American Democracy* (Jackson, MS: U. Press of Mississippi, 1982; p. 57), "Morning programming is dominated by game shows which project blatant materialistic greed; afternoons offer soap opera involving various sorts of depravity; and nighttime television sketches an image of sit-com inanity or crime show brutality. Interspersed throughout, commercials present vacuous housewives, a drug-dependent people, and those who define life by material possessions and sexual conquests."

21. According to *Frequently Asked Questions About Public Broadcasting* (Washington, DC: Corporation for Public Broadcasting, 1995), in 1993 the United States spent $1.09 per citizen on public television, while Canada spent $31.05, Japan spent $32.02, and Great Britain spent $38.99. See J. Ledbetter, *Made Possible By . . . The Death of Public Broadcasting in the United States* (New York and London: Verso, 1997), p. 4.

22. R. McChesney, *Corporate Media and the Threat to Democracy* (New York: Seven Stories Press, 1997), pp. 6-7. McChesney adds: "Fewer than ten colossal vertically integrated media conglomerates now dominate U.S. media. The five largest firms—with annual sales in the $10-25 billion range—are News Corporation, Time Warner, Disney, Viacom, and TCI. These firms are major producers of entertainment and media software and have distribution networks like television networks, cable channels and retail stores. Time Warner, for example, owns music recording studios, film and television production studios, several cable television channels, cable broadcasting systems,

amusement parks, the WB television network, book publishing houses, magazine publishing interests, retail stores, motion picture theaters, and much else." (p. 18). See also: Ben Bagdikian, *The Media Monopoly* (Boston: Beacon Press, 1987); Robert Cirino, *Don't Blame the People* (New York: Random House, 1972); and *The Nation*, June 3, 1996.

23. For a brief account of this conservative propaganda machine, see R. Parry, "Lost History: Rise of the Right-Wing Machine," *The Consortium* 1:26 (Nov. 25, 1996): 3-5. David Callahan of the Century Foundation estimates that, "spending by the top twenty conservative think tanks will likely top $1 billion in the nineties." (D. Callahan, "$1 Billion for Conservative Ideas," *The Nation*, April 26, 1999, p. 21).

24. Quoted in J. Weisman, "Public Interest & Private Greed," *Columbia Journalism Review* (May/June 1990): 46.

25. Quoted in J. Cohen, "TV Industry Wields Power in DC," *Baltimore Sun*, May 4, 1997.

26. E.E. Dennis, "How 'Liberal' Are the Media, Anyway?" *Harvard International Journal of Press/Politics* 2:4 (Fall 1997): 118.

27. M. Hertsgaard, *On Bended Knee: The Press and the Reagan Presidency*. (New York: Schocken Books, 1988, 1989): p. 77.

28. R. Darnton, *The Kiss of Lamourette: Reflections in Cultural History* (New York: W.W. Norton, 1990), pp. 76-77.

29. Austin Ranney, *Channels of Power: The Impact of Television on American Politics* (New York: Basic Books, 1983), p. 51. Epstein's interviews in the 1970s with dozens of TV correspondents, producers, and technicians in the early 1970s support this view (see: E.J. Epstein, *News from Nowhere: Television and the News* [New York: Random House, 1973], and Epstein, "The Values of Newsmen," *Television Quarterly* 10:2 [Winter 1973]: 9-20). Of the 32 cor-

respondents Epstein spoke with, he reported (p. 12) that "More than two thirds denied ever having registered as a member of a political party." As a senior network executive told him, "It is simply not in our enlightened self-interest to employ reporters with too firmly fixed ideas on how the world ought to be."

30. See M. Dolny, "The Think Tank Spectrum: For the Media, Some Thinkers are More Equal than Others," *Extra!* 9:3 (May/June 1996): 21.

31. As Eric Alterman observes in *Sound and Fury: The Washington Punditocracy and the Collapse of American Politics* (New York: HarperCollins, 1992), the moderate David Broder is "the only non-right-wing pundit who begins to challenge the circulation numbers" of columnists such as George F. Will, William Safire, James J. Kilpatrick, and Patrick Buchanan.

32. J. Lewis and M. Morgan, "Issues, Images & Impact: A FAIR Survey of Voters' Knowledge," *Extra!* (Dec. 1992): 11.

33. According to a 1993 poll by the Times Mirror Center for the People and the Press, talk radio shows distort public opinion because people who call in to such shows constitute a largely conservative "vocal minority." Forty-five percent of callers, for example, had an unfavorable opinion of President Clinton, compared to 35 percent of the general public. See R.L. Berke, "Poll Says Conservatives Dominate Talk Radio," *The New York Times*, July 16, 1993, p. A12.

34. Quoted in R.D. Elving, "On Radio, All Politics Is a Lot Less Vocal," *Congressional Quarterly Weekly Report* (May 10, 1997): 1102.

35. M. Lerner, *The Politics of Meaning: Restoring Hope and Possibility in an Age of Cynicism* (New York: Addison–Wesley, 1996), p. 83.

36. E.J. Dionne, Jr., *They Only Look Dead: Why Progressives Will Dominate the Next Political Era* (New York: Simon & Schuster, 1996), p. 256.

37. Replayed on "Illusions of News" (1989), a segment of the 4 part PBS series *The Public Mind: Image and Reality in America with Bill Moyers.*

38. The 1990 tax revolt in New Jersey provides a case in point. Democratic Governor James Florio had raised taxes to comply with a state Supreme Court ruling mandating that poorer school districts be funded at the same level as wealthier ones. The revolt began with a call-in to a talk radio show on WKXW-FM, a station in Trenton. The tinder used by the station to feed the flame included using a soundtrack of pig noises and the theme song from the movie *Jaws.* The result: an antitax political firestorm that swept many Democrats, including Florio, from office. (See M. Hoyt, "Talk Radio: Turning Up the Volume," *Columbia Journalism Review* [Nov.–Dec. 1992]: 47. Hoyt notes that several hundred talk radio shows get suggestions of talking points and guest lists from the right-of-center National Forum Foundation.)

39. One reason for the demise of mainstream religious shows was an FCC ruling in 1960 that the mandatory public service time provided by stations need not be "sustaining," or free, time. In other words, station owners could get public service credit for time sold to religious broadcasters, so there was no longer any reason to give it away. This ruling helped pave the way for the electronic ministries, which were willing and able to pay for air time.

40. Robert Abelman, and Gary Pettey, "How Political Is Religious Television?" *Journalism Quarterly* 65:2 (1988): 359.

41. See D.H. Bennett, *The Party of Fear: The American Far*

Right from Nativism to the Militia Movement (New York: Vintage Books, 1995), p. 383.

42. See J. Hadden, "The Rise and Fall of American Televangelism," *Annals of the American Academy of Political and Social Science*, 527 (May 1993): p. 120. Hadden further notes that "The ancillary projects of the televangelists, including cathedrals, colleges and universities, religious theme parks, and total-living communities, also grew at a phenomenal pace."

43. G. Knight, "The Reality Effects of Tabloid Television," in M. Raboy & P.A. Bruck, eds., *Communication For and Against Democracy* (Montreal and New York: Black Rose Books, 1989), pp. 123–124.

44. See *Extra! Update*, bimonthly newsletter of FAIR, Oct. 1997.

45. In true corporate "Alice in Wonderland" style, NBC defended the hiring of Rivera as partly motivated by the fear that a rival, Fox News, might hire him and thereby gain "credibility."

46. A. Heyward, "The Seven Daily Sins of Television News" *Television Quarterly* 28:4 (1997): 71-75.

Chapter II

1. I use the term 'reality' in quotation marks to acknowledge the philosophic complexity of the term, which I don't propose to explore here. However one might wish to embroider or qualify it, we use the term in ordinary speech for the same reason that all metaphysical judgements are made: communicative practicality.

2. K. Lang, and G.E. Lang, "The Unique Perspective of Television and its Effect: A Pilot Study," *American Sociological Review* 18:1 (Feb. 1953): 3-12. This pioneering article on television's effects looks exclusively at the 1953 MacArthur Day parade in Chicago.

3. I. Pichel, "Seeing with the Camera," *Hollywood Quarterly* 1 (1945–46): 142.

4. S. Smith, *Sam Smith's Great American Political Repair Manual* (New York: W.W. Norton, 1997), p. 193.

5. Many of these characteristics apply variously to radio, film, video games, and other media. But there are important differences, some obvious and others (e.g., regarding their respective economics) too far afield to be addressed here. For a fuller account of these valences of television, see J. Mander, *Four Arguments for the Elimination of Television*, Ch. 16. Mander finds thirty-three distinct biases in the structure of television. Although the roster of biases I am suggesting is not directly based on Mander's argument, I don't think the overlap is accidental.

6. G. Knight, "The Reality Effects of Tabloid Television News," in M. Raboy and P.A. Bruck, eds., *Communication For and Against Democracy*, 119. Another TV analyst, Edmund Carpenter, notes that, "Readers experience a necessity to translate images into flesh and statements into actions. Television, by contrast, seems complete in itself.... Concepts such as causation and purpose appear irrelevant, basic only to the thinking of the past." ("Reality and Television: an Interview with Dr. Edmund Carpenter," *Television Quarterly* 10:1 [Fall 1972]: 44).

7. Ranney, *Channels of Power*, p. 73.

8. "The age-old problem of democracy," writes John Birt (*TV Guide*, Aug. 9, 1975, p. 6) "is aggravated [by TV] because the media in their present forms instinctively fasten onto the snags and drawbacks in any proposed new policy. Television normally communicates these more effectively than the policy as a whole or, indeed, than the overall problem to be solved."

9. J. Fiske, and J. Hartley, *Reading Television* (London: Methuen, 1978), p. 15; quoted in L. Langsdorf, "Dialogue, Distanciation, and Engagement: Toward a Logic of Televisual Communication," *Informal Logic* 10:3 (Fall 1988). It has been suggested that even the perception that television is "easier" than print may have a self-fulfilling tendency to lessen the investment of mental effort, and in turn, inferential learning. See G. Salomon, "Television Is 'Easy' and Print Is 'Tough': The Differential Investment of Mental Effort in Learning as a Function of Perceptions and Attributes," *Journal of Educational Psychology* 76:4 (1984): 647–658.

10. S. Vanocur, *Nieman Reports* 44:5 (Winter-2, 1990): 28–29.

11. Visual display of information doesn't always militate against abstraction; for example, certain topological and other mathematical concepts are conveyed most effectively through images. But such images don't always provide a complete understanding; they may be important tools of comprehension rather than the end result.

12. D. L. Paletz, & R. M. Entman, *Media Power and Politics* (New York: The Free Press, 1981), 17.

13. Roderick P. Hart, *Seducing America: How Television Charms the Modern Voter* (New York: Oxford U. Press, 1994), 86.

14. T. Gitlin, *Inside Prime Time* (New York: Pantheon Books, 1985), p. 270. See also Austin Ranney, *Channels of Power*, pp. 55–56.

15. Gerbner, "Television: the New State Religion?" *Et cetera* 24:2 (June 1977): 145.

16. J. Bourdon, "Television and Political Memory" (trans. by J. Waley), *Media, Culture and Society* 14:4 (Oct. 1992): 542.

17. Sontag, "In Plato's Cave," *On Photography* (New York: Farrar, Straus & Giroux, 1977); Doubleday/Anchor Books, 1990, pp. 22–23.

18. The average TV sound bite of statements by presidential candidates shrank from 42.3 seconds in 1968 to 8.4 seconds in 1992. Other researchers have come up with nearly identical figures. A study by Dennis T. Lowry and Jon A. Schidler ("The Sound Bites, the Biters, and the Bitten: An Analysis of Network TV News Bias in Campaign '92," *Journalism and Mass Communication Quarterly* 72:1 [Spring 1995]: 33–44) shows that the shrinking has stopped, undoubtedly due to a "floor effect." According to Lowry and Shidler (pp. 35–37), sound bites (defined somewhat narrowly as "all statements made on the air by news sources," constituted 29.8 percent of total story time on network news, or roughly seven of the twenty-two minutes that comprise the typical news hole.

19. *The New Republic*, May 28, 1990. A concomitant of this process has been the proliferation of TV news stories about how politicians manipulate TV news. Paradoxically, such stories provide a measure of self-critical analysis, yet also reflect just how manipulable television is—and the importance of such manipulation in modern politics.

20. This is often a cooperative act of the subject and the medium; as Adam Clymer noted in *The New York Times* ("Extreme Rhetoric Bedevils Congress," June 25, 1995, p. A16), " . . . almost all debate [in the US Senate] is for sound bites, fed by the hope that network television will use an extreme comment. Most members speak as if they think that not one of their colleagues is listening seriously—or could be persuaded by thoughtful arguments."

21. *The Age of Indifference: A Study of Young Americans and How They View the News* (Washington, DC: Times Mirror Center for The People & The Press, 1990).

22. Kurtz, *Hot Air*, pp. 9, 367.

23. C. Lasch, *The Revolt of the Elites and the Betrayal of Democracy* (New York: W.W. Norton, 1995), p. 162. Public misconceptions, furthermore (presumably based on media accounts) often reflect a conservative bias. For example, the portion of the US budget that goes to foreign aid and the cost of domestic social programs are widely and vastly overestimated. "Heavy TV viewers were often less well informed than light TV viewers" reports Justin Lewis ("What Do We Learn From the News?" *Extra!* Sept. 1992: 16-17.) See also: J. Lewis and M. Morgan, "Issues, Images & Impact: A FAIR Survey of Voters' Knowledge," *Extra!* (Dec. 1992): 7-11; and on foreign aid, social security, and medical care, James Fallows, *Breaking the News*, pp. 167–168.

24. E.g., one might question the narrow distinction in Lasch's claim (*op. cit.*, p. 162) that "It is the decay of public debate, not the school system (bad as it is) that makes the public ill informed, notwithstanding the wonders of the age of information."

25. Exceptions include certain protracted courtroom dramas, such as the O.J. Simpson trial, which assumed spectacular proportions through television, in part due to its highly symbolic nature as a morality play about race, wealth, and celebrity.

26. Quoted in Paletz & Entman, *op. cit.*, p. 17.

27. See, e.g., Tim Golden, "Crime Rates May Be Down, but the Problem Stays Hot with Politicians, Voters," *The New York Times*, Sept 22, 1996, p. A26. Golden reports that, "People's views on the issue, experts say, appear to be shaped much more by what they see on their local television news and the movies, by the talk

at their workplaces and by the politicians" than by actual statistics.

28. Mander, *Four Arguments for the Elimination of Television*, p. 328.

29. Bourdieu, *On Television* (trans. by P.P. Furgeson; New York: The New Press, 1998), p. 7.

Chapter III

1. M. Arlen, *The View from Highway 1* (New York: Farrar, Straus & Giroux, 1976), p. 9.

2. I am using 'reality' in the ordinary sense, to mean the aggregate of directly perceived and mediated experiences. It would seem a merely semantic question whether we call television land a form of unreality, a subset of reality, or an alternate reality. The paramount fact is that TV is parasitic on objective reality but seldom if ever perfectly faithful to it, and the two spheres blur in our minds.

3. J.D. Peters, "Information: Notes Toward a Critical History," *Journal of Communication Inquiry* 12:2 (Summer 1988): 15.

4. (Barthes) Interview, *Le Photographe* (Feb. 1980); in *Roland Barthes: The Grain of the Voice: Interviews 1962-1980*, trans. by L. Coverdale (Berkeley & Los Angeles: U. of California Press, 1991), p. 354.

5. See, for example, R. Andersen, "That's Entertainment: How 'Reality'-Based Crime Shows Market Police Brutality," *Extra!* 7:3 (May/June 1994): 15–16: "Themes of prevention, education and the elimination of poverty have no place in 'reality'-based crime shows . . . . The absence of economic context on these programs, together with the approval of the excessive use of force,

creates a 'law-and-order' ideology that promises that public safety . . . can be achieved without addressing such underlying issues as racial conflict, education and poverty."

6. Quoted by James Sterngold, "Seeking to Go Beyond the Shockumentary," *The New York Times*, Jan. 25, 1999, p. E6.

7. D.L. Paletz, & R.M. Entman, *Media Power and Politics*, p. 180.

8. "Part of a Talk," *Television Quarterly* 6:4 (Fall 1967): 41.

9. Quoted by Michael DeSousa in "The Emerging Self-Portrait: The Television of Television," *Journal of Popular Film and Video* 9:3 (Fall 1981): 147.

10. M. Pei, "Blurred Vision: The Disturbing Impact of Electronic Media" *Change* 8:10 (Nov. 1976): p. 44.

11. B. Seitz, "The Televised and the Untelevised: Keeping an Eye On/Off the Tube," in H.J. Silverman, ed., *Continental Philosophy III: Postmodernism—Philosophy and the Arts* (New York: Routledge, 1990), p. 205.

12. I. Glasser, "Television and the Construction of Reality," *Et cetera* 45:2 (Summer 1988): 156–162.

13. Glasser, *op. cit.*, p. 158.

14. Bill McKibben, "TV or Not TV," *The New York Times* (May 27, 1992), p. A21.

15. Mander, *Four Arguments for the Elimination of Television*, p. 246.

16. G.R. Funkhouser & E.F. Shaw, "How Synthetic Experience Shapes Reality," *Journal of Communication* 40:2 (Spring 1990), pp. 78–79.

17. Funkhouser and Shaw, *op. cit.*, p. 82.

18. See Daniel J. Boorstin, *The Image: A Guide to Pseudo-*

Events in America (25th anniversary edition, New York: Random House, 1987), p. 250. The ad shows a man in a parked Chevrolet at the edge of what appears to be the Grand Canyon, looking into a portable slide viewer.

19. P. Conrad, *Television: The Medium and Its Manners* (London: Routledge & Kegan Paul, 1982), p. 170.

20. Introduction, *Past Imperfect: History According to the Movies*, ed. T. Mico *et al.*, (New York: Henry Holt, 1995), p. 9.

21. For example, the 1979 ABC miniseries *Ike* mythologized Gen. Dwight D. Eisenhower, simplified his character and those of other major figures, and dwelt on his relationship with his aide, Kay Summersby. As James Combs notes, " . . . we never see the larger forces at work which surround and impel the action. TV can focus on Ike and Kay holding hands, but not on the 101st Airborne Division, much less the meaning of fascism." ("Television Aesthetics and the Depiction of Heroism: The Case of the TV Historical Biography," *Journal of Popular Film and Television* 8:2 (1980), 17).

22. E. Foner, "The Televised Past," *Television Quarterly* 16:2 (Summer 1979): 62.

23. For example, *Great Escapes of World War II*, broadcast on A&E in 1997. Although actual footage of great events—particularly high-level or secret wartime deliberations—is often unavailable or nonexistent, certain rules of authenticity cannot be waived in the name of art or commerce, especially given television's mass audience. As one writer has sensibly put it, "So far as actuality material is concerned, the most important rule is not to pretend that material shot at a particular time and place was shot at a different time and in another place." (J. Kuehl, "Television History: The Next Step," *Sight and Sound* 51:3 (Summer 1982): 189).

24. Just as professional scholarship may be erudite to the point of irrelevance, mass mediated history may, by pandering to audience expectations and commercial imperatives, present an oversimplified or compromised picture, e.g., by stressing familiar or popular themes and safe interpretations.

25. For an excellent discussion of "[t]he dramatic tricks and rearrangements of reality which are necessary to create television reality" see Brian Rose's "Mass Mediated Images: The Force of Television in *The China Syndrome*," *Journal of Popular Film and Television* (Fall 1980): 2-9.

26. See, for example, J. Gleick, "Reality Check," *The New York Times Magazine*, May 17, 1997; also Amy M. Spindler, "Making the Camera Lie, Digitally and Often," *The New York Times*, June 17, 1997, p. B7.

27. S. Prince, "True Lies: Perceptual Realism, Digital Images, and Film Theory" *Film Quarterly* 49:3 (Spring 1996): 27-37.

28. "Given video technology, morphing, transposition, texture mapping, and modeling sequences, we need to anticipate a revolutionary play of image substitutions which accepts that representations are variable and that visual displays, not linear narrative conventions, transmit evolving information. This will destabilize and contaminate film images and the fantasies they structure." (F.G. See, "Something Reflective," *Journal of Popular Film and Television* 22:4 [Winter 1995]: 170).

Chapter IV

1. (Gramsci) in D. Forgacs and G. Nowell-Smith, eds., *Antonio Gramsci: Selections from the Cultural Writings* (translated by W. Boelhower; Cambridge: Harvard U. Press, 1991), p. 417.

2. See, for example, G. Johnson, "Researchers on Complexity

Ponder What It's All About," *The New York Times*, May 7, 1997, pp. C1, C7.

3. L. Hendrickson, "Media Reliance and Complexity of Perspective of International Relations" *Journalism Quarterly* 66:4 (Winter 1989): 876–877. In her study, Hendrickson finds a significant, but not strong, correlation between reliance on newspapers for international news and the complexity of one's outlook. She finds a stronger correlation between reliance on television news and a "negative effect on complexity" (p. 880).

4. "Environment" is a locus of complexity in several senses of the word: the natural environment; the logical or definitional environment in which an idea or concept is understood; and the background conditions—causal, contextual, descriptive—surrounding an action, event, situation, problem, etc. Environments are general fields of reference to which specific objects (persons, events, situations, processes, etc.) are relatable: natural, logical, or descriptive systems. Specific objects are invariably simpler when considered out-of-context or isolated from their environments. Because television is scene-bound, it is inept at reproducing environments or reflecting their importance.

5. Todd R. La Porte writes that, "The degree of complexity of organized social systems . . . is a function of the number of system components . . . the relative differentiation or variety of these components . . . and the degree of interdependence among these components. . . ." La Porte, ed., *Organized Social Complexity: Challenge to Politics and Policy* (Princeton, NJ: Princeton University Press, 1975), p. 6.

6. The Cold War and its aftermath have exacerbated these differences, while also skewing and complicating them. Hence the irony of a Democratic president's aggressively pursuing eco-

nomic goals in China policy, as congressional conservatives push for a harder stand against China on human rights.

7. This view traces back to Plato's attack on poetry in Book X of *The Republic*. See A. Nehamas, "Plato and the Mass Media," *The Monist* 71 (April 1988): 214-234.

8. See, e.g., J.G. Blumler, & M. Gurevitch, "The Political Effects of Mass Communications" in M. Gurevitch et al., eds., *Culture, Society and the Media* (New York and London: Routledge, 1990).

9. ibid., p. 258.

10. See, e.g., Albert Borgmann, *Technology and the Character of Contemporary Life: A Philosophical Inquiry* (Chicago: U. of Chicago Press, 1984), p. 60; and Langdon Winner, "Three Paradoxes of the Information Age" in G. Bender & T. Druckrey, eds., *Culture on the Brink: Ideologies of Technology* (Seattle: Bay Press, 1994).

11. A. Borgmann, "The Moral Assessment of Technology," in Langdon Winner, ed., *Democracy in a Technological Society.* (Dordrecht: Kluwer Academic Publishers, 1992), p. 209.

12. N. Postman, *Amusing Ourselves to Death: Public Discourse in the Age of Show Business* (New York: Viking Penguin, 1985), p. 31.

13. See T. Streeter, "Selling the Air: Property and the Politics of U.S. Commercial Broadcasting," *Media Culture & Society* 10 (Jan. 1994): 91–116.

14. R.T. Craig, "Why Are There So *Many* Communication Theories?" *Journal of Communication* 43:3 (Summer 1993): 31.

15. Religious doctrines are often based in moral conservatism and simplicity; but the spiritual impulse and the complexitarian are alike, and contrast with television, in subordinating the visible. In *Moby-Dick*, Ishmael is a man of the spirit, reflecting

before going to sea: "Methinks my body is but the lees of my better being . . . and come a stove boat and stove body when they
will, for stave my soul, Jove himself cannot." Ahab is more of a
complexitarian, haunted by invisible but immanent powers. He
shouts from "The Quarter-Deck" that "All visible objects, man,
are but as pasteboard masks," and later declares: "All the things
that most exasperate and outrage mortal man . . . are bodiless, but
only bodiless as objects, not as agents. There's a most special, a
most cunning, oh, a most malicious difference!"

16. Morris R. Cohen's doctrine of polarity also expresses the
idea that opposites, "like the . . . poles of a magnet, all involve
each other when applied to any significant entity." *Reason and
Nature: An Essay on the Meaning of Scientific Method* (New
York: Harcourt Brace, 1931), p. 165; see also ch. 4 of *A Preface to
Logic* (New York: Henry Holt, 1944).

17. A definitive treatment of this subject is R. Bambrough's
"Aristotle on Justice: A Paradigm of Philosophy" in Bambrough,
ed., *New Essays on Plato and Aristotle* (London: Routledge &
Kegan Paul, 1965).

18. The more complex vision corresponds to what Sonia
Hoffman, the physicist character portrayed by Liv Ullman in the
1991 film *Mindwalk*, calls "ecological thinking." It eschews rigid
polarities, isolates, and causal monism (and the idea of the present as an isolated point in time) in favor of larger conceptual
frameworks: systems, processes, relationships, and concern for the
future. Not surprisingly, *Mindwalk* is a slow-moving film, more
dialogic than theatrical or cinematic, and ill-suited to commercial television.

19. Bobbio, *Left and Right*, p. 92.

20. Dionne, *They Only Look Dead*, p. 256.

21. Levi, *The Drowned and the Saved*, trans. by R. Rosenthal (New York: Summit Books, 1986), pp. 36–37.

22. Solomon, *Narcissism and Intimacy* (New York: W.W. Norton, 1989), p. 46.

23. Donald M. Kaplan, "Psychopathology of Television Watching" *Intellectual Digest* (November 1972): 27.

24. J. Mander, *Four Arguments for the Elimination of Television*, p. 168.

25. See, for example, E. Frenkel-Brunswik, "Intolerance of Ambiguity as an Emotional and Perceptual Personality Variable," *Journal of Personality* 18 (1949): 108-141. Works by T. Adorno *et al.* on *The Authoritarian Personality* (New York: Harper, 1950), and M. Rokeach, *The Open and Closed Mind: Investigations into the Nature of Belief Systems and Personality Systems* (New York: Basic Books, 1960) have also suggested links between certain personality types and a tendency to view the world in terms of rigid polarities. In addition, a range of thinkers, including J. Piaget, L. Kohlberg, A. Korzybski, M. Basseches, and R. Lauer, have postulated discrete stages in the development of cognition and moral awareness marked by increasing complexity. See, e.g., Lauer's essay on adult development in M.F. Levy, ed., *Research and Theory in Developmental Psychology* (New York: Irvington, 1983).

26. L. Bobo, & F.C. Licari, "Education and Political Tolerance," *Public Opinion Quarterly* 53:3 (Fall 1989): 303.

27. One might imagine a society in which the reverse were true: i.e., in which citizens were guaranteed basic economic equality (or some forms of it), but their respective rights to political equality were left to the economic marketplace. There is an element of this in the influence of economic interests (such as political action committees) in a political system. The reason why we

don't find such societies is the primacy of political order in constituting society and determining the extent and balance of both political and economic rights.

28. While political discourse is not philosophical discourse, it is almost always a shadow of it: political issues invariably reflect deeper contentions of moral and political principles.

29. In its complexity, one might argue, liberal theory fails to reduce to simple first principles as compellingly as conservatism. But conservatism arguably has the converse defect: in its intellectual simplicity it fails to account for the complexity of human society.

30. A. France, *Le Lys Rouge*, 1894.

31. I don't use the term 'artificial' pejoratively. All human inventions are artificial by definition, and many are morally innocuous in and of themselves (although a complexitarian would dispute whether they can be dissociated from their social functions).

32. Second presidential debate, San Diego, CA., Oct. 16, 1996.

33. Commencement speech at Howard University, June 4, 1964; quoted in D. P. Moynihan, *Family and Nation* (New York: Harcourt Brace Jovanovich, 1986), p. 31.

34. This is an example of what we might call the Principle of Appropriation. A more complex view can often be understood as appropriating an area of thought or action to regulate, explain, analyze, etc., which the simpler view either ignores or refuses to invest with moral or intellectual significance. This principle restates the numerical definition of complexity: a moral or intellectual framework that addresses a question or domain of questions which a rival framework ignores is a fortiori more complex.

35. This is not to deny the important areas of convergence in

the Judeo-Christian tradition and in most social and religious codes, e.g., in condemning murder and other heinous crimes. But that convergence is hardly complete, nor has it been sufficient to prevent genocide, slavery, child labor, or sundry other atrocities. Likewise, tolerance is only an issue where codes or practices conflict, but those conflicts are often significant and fierce.

36. Two of the prominent social issues on the American agenda, abortion and gun control, do not directly assimilate to the tolerance framework. But they do reflect divergent thresholds of complexity, with corresponding implications for the role of government in regulating individual conduct. Gun control is in fact a paradigmatic conflict between a simpler conception of individual freedom, in which autonomy is maximized regardless of the consequences for other agents, and a more complex view in which autonomy is limited for the protection of others. A case in point: the National Rifle Association recently produced a series of ads aimed at children, featuring cartoon characters such as "Eddie Eagle," purporting to teach gun safety. Critics on the left, such as the Violence Policy Center, have contended that the ads are really designed to normalize gun ownership in children's minds, in order to prepare a future market for fire arms, and to forestall legislation mandating trigger locks on guns.

37. This is partly for obvious economic reasons, i.e., television's need to placate a broader audience. But it is also easier to spew invective in a medium that doesn't show one's face.

38. A 1982 study indirectly supports this supposition, finding that children's school achievement improved as TV viewing increased up to about ten hours per week, but declined at higher levels. (P.A. Williams, et al., "The Impact of Leisure-time Tele-

vision on School Learning: A Research Synthesis," *American Educational Research Journal* 19 [1982]: 19-50.)

39. S. Diamond, *Not by Politics Alone: The Enduring Influence of the Christian Right* (New York: The Guilford Press, 1998), p. 27.

40. It doesn't matter here that "nature" is itself an abstraction which, in the strictest sense, we cannot observe without altering it, or that subatomic particles behave with evident randomness. As a practical matter, we cannot comprehend the supra-atomic world of ordinary experience and stable objects except in Newtonian terms of discernible causes and effects. Discerning those causes and effects is the essence of the scientific enterprise if not the basis of consciousness itself. While Werner Heisenberg was right about the unpredictability of subatomic particles, Newton was right about apples: they still fall on your head. Like most science, ordinary experience is predicated on our understanding of nature (but not human nature) as being rigidly deterministic.

41. At least, this is true to the extent that the "social sciences" are properly modeled on the same logical and quantitative rigor as science itself. In what sense these disciplines should presume to be scientific, and whether their rigor depends on that presumption, is another matter.

42. On the episodic character of television, see Shanto Iyengar, *Is Anyone Responsible?: How Television Frames Political Issues.* (Chicago: U. of Chicago Press, 1991).

43. I am not suggesting that conservatives in every sense have a simpler view of the world. Norberto Bobbio notes that "Awareness of the complexity of reality" is an aspect of conservative thought (*Left and Right*, p. 46). However, this is not only different from axiological, or value-related, complexity; if anything, they are in a converse relationship. Thus, some on the left, in their

zeal for change, may exaggerate the ease of effecting it, while some on the right may cite the complexity of social reality, and exaggerate the difficulty of effecting change in their zeal to forestall it.

44. A. Gopnik, "Read All About It," *The New Yorker*, Dec. 12, 1994: 96.

45. The classic essay on the subject of essential contestability is W.B. Gallie's "Essentially Contested Concepts," *Proceedings of the Aristotelian Society* 56 (1955-56): 167-198. See also A. MacIntyre, "The Essential Contestability of Some Social Concepts," *Ethics* 84 (1973): 1-9; E. Garver, "Essentially Contested Concepts: The Ethics and Tactics of Argument," *Philosophy and Rhetoric* 23:4 (1990): 251-270; and E. Garver, "Rhetoric and Essentially Contested Arguments," *Philosophy and Rhetoric* 11:3 (1978): 156-172.

Chapter V

1. "Informal logic examines the nature and function of arguments in natural language," and thus it "widens the scope [of formal logic] to include inductive as well as deductive patterns of inference." T. Honderich, *The Oxford Companion to Philosophy* (New York: Oxford University Press, 1995).

2. Polemical or otherwise uncritical thinking is typically characterized by various related lapses, including the failure to observe:

1) Important distinctions within ideas or categories (e.g., "special interests" as public vs. private interests).

2) Connections between nominally distinct ideas or categories.

3) Rigidly binary thinking that ignores spectrums or gradations.

4) Differences between ideas and what they represent.

5) Meanings, assumptions, conflicts, interests, motives, etc., that might weaken or alter an argument.

6) Intolerance of ambiguity, and of contrasting but coexisting facts or ideas; failure to distinguish between ambiguity and contradiction; failure to recognize how differences and identities may overlap.

3. Conservative appeals to strict construction typically overlook the fact that rights don't exist in a moral-political vacuum; they compete with other rights, and entail correlative duties. Thus, their denial implicitly ascribes countervailing rights to others.

4. This is not the place to address the intractable issue of abortion. But it is relevant to observe that the reasoning behind *Roe v. Wade* — using the trimesters of pregnancy as arbitrary but reasonable legal boundaries for competing claims where none exist in nature — is more complex than arguments that reduce abortion to either "choice" or "murder."

5. See A. Silverblatt, *Media Literacy: Keys to Interpreting Media Messages* (Westport, CT: Praeger, 1995), p. 262.

6. Attacking nonprofit "special interests" while defending powerful private lobbies is a glaring example of conservative humbug. As the editors of *Extra!* wrote to *The New York Times* (letter to the editor, Oct. 16, 1987; *Extra!* [Jan./Feb. 1992, p. 26]): "In the past, the term 'special interests' was usually affixed to private economic interests that relied on dollars instead of numbers of supporters to exercise undue power over political and governmental institutions. . . . Needless to say, Reagan/Bush policies that dramatically transferred wealth from working people to the wealthy are not described as 'class warfare.'"

7. Jerry Mander argues similarly in *Four Arguments for the Elimination of Television*, pp. 337–340.

8. TV is also blinkered to the more diffuse and cumulative effects of conservative policies, such as the mounting deficit of the Reagan-Bush Era.

9. Kate Moody, "Growing Media Smarts—The New Mexico Project" *Media Studies Journal* 8:4 (Fall 1994): 147.

10. "Critical Thinking in the Electronic Era," *The National Forum* 65 (Winter 1985): 8.

11. More specifically, media literacy promotes critical awareness in several dimensions: in society (the different capacities and limitations of various media, and modes of their evaluation); in the organization of knowledge (different types and functions of information, understanding, and skills); and in personal skills-development and self-awareness, through production experience and understanding how personal media consumption competes with other social and asocial activities.

12. For an interesting critique of media literacy pedagogy and theory, see D. Buckingham, "Television Literacy: A Critique," *Radical Philosophy* 51 (Spring 1989): 12-25.

13. Nevertheless, in debates about the scope of democracy itself, conservatives tend to take narrower positions than liberals.

14. Similarly, in the House Bank "scandal," most Americans erroneously believed that the overdrafts were illegal; that they involved public monies; and that they involved a real bank, and not a financial cooperative and payroll office.

15. E.J. Dionne, Jr., *They Only Look Dead: Why Progressives Will Dominate the Next Political Era*, p. 250.

16. N.R. Luttbeg and M.M. Gant, for example, find that while about 80 percent of those voters who identified the terms 'liberal' and 'conservative' did so correctly in a 1980 study, "about two out of five respondents could not venture a description of these

words." ["The Failure of Liberal/ Conservative Ideology as a Cognitive Structure," *Public Opinion Quarterly* 49:1 (Spring 1985): 84].

17. There are certain exceptions where significant consensus can be achieved, such as basic adherence to democratic norms and matters of national security. But as noted in Chapter IV, even these are rarely without some ideological shading.

18. "Information," Lasch adds, "usually seen as the precondition of debate, is better understood as its by-product. When we get into arguments that focus and fully engage our attention, we become avid seekers of relevant information. Otherwise we take in information passively—if we take it in at all." (*The Revolt of the Elites*, pp. 162–3).

19. Dionne, *op. cit.*, p. 257.

20. It doesn't make viewers less cynical when politics, media, and celebrity are conflated, and their respective skills and purposes are treated as irrelevant or interchangeable, if it increases the audience share. A glaring example was CBS News's hiring of Susan Molinari in 1997 as a co-host for *CBS News Saturday Morning*. (Many others have made the transition from activist to commentator, but not the more awkward one from elected official to prominent anchor-person.) Ironically, Ms. Molinari's visible inexperience as a TV anchor underscored the very skills broadcasting requires, much as Michael Jordan showed that not all great athletes can play baseball.

21. Cynicism and the corresponding aversion to serious or critical thinking are not confined to the electronic media. Take, for example, President Clinton's remark in a 1997 speech that "A lot of brilliant people . . . believe that the nation-state is fast becoming a relic of the past." Instead of examining that important idea,

a *New York Times* reporter sneered that the president was exploring "vague theoretical byways." (James Bennet, "President Using Fund-Raising Speeches to Test Campaign Themes for '98," *The New York Times*, Nov. 25, 1997, p. A20.)

22. G. Knight, "The Reality Effects of Tabloid Television" in M. Raboy and P.A. Bruck, eds., *Communication For and Against Democracy*, p. 127.

23. Knight seems to come close to recognizing this, adding that the problem of progressive media is one of "resubordinating form to substance in a manner that breaks with the consensualism of current television practice without losing the critical edge of its populism." If the form cannot be changed, the content and political-economic structure can.

24. E.g., "When the Allies occupied post-war Japan and Germany, they were careful to prohibit [media] consolidation, noting that too-concentrated media markets were antidemocratic and promoted fascism." (Mark Crispin Miller and Robert W. McChesney, "Cut the Media Giants Down to Size," *Newsday*, Oct. 15, 1997, p. A41.)

25. P. Charren, "'As I told the FCC . . .': Yet Another Modest Proposal for Children's Television," *Media Studies Journal* 8:4 (Fall 1994): 14.

26. Speech at Princeton University; quoted in *Channeling Influence: The Broadcast Lobby and the $70 Billion Free Ride* (Washington, DC: Common Cause, 1997), p. 30.

27. These suggestions, in various forms, have been made by Ben Bagdikian, Lawrence K. Grossman, Mark Crispin Miller, Robert W. McChesney, Danny Schechter, and others.

28. See, for example, Kathleen M. Sullivan of Stanford University, "The Role of the Media in Representative Government,"

in *New Federalist Papers: Essays in Defense of the Constitution* (New York: W.W. Norton/Twentieth Century Fund, 1997).

29. See R.W. McChesney, "Off the Spectrum," *Extra!* 10:4 (July/August 1997): p. 16.

30. Grossman, "In the Public Interest: How to Escape from a Highway Robbery," *Columbia Journalism Review* (Sept./Oct. 1997): 58; see also Grossman, *The Electronic Republic: Reshaping Democracy in the Information Age* (New York: Viking, 1995).

31. J. Ledbetter, *Made Possible By . . .* , p. 235.

32. While all advertising is manipulative, some forms are more blatantly contrary to the public interest. Thus, tobacco advertising has been formally banned from TV, and liquor advertising informally. Ads aimed at children are clearly exploitive and compromise the discretion of parents, just as ads for prescription drugs compromise the discretion of physicians.

33. "La Crise Permanente," *Pouvoirs*, No. 18 (1981): 6; quoted in Perry Anderson, "The Affinities of Norberto Bobbio," *New Left Review* 170 (July–Aug. 1988): p. 10; also in P. Anderson, *A Zone of Engagement* (London and New York: Verso, 1992).

Selected Bibliography

Adorno, T. "How to Look at Television." *Quarterly of Film, Radio and Television* 8 (1953–54): 213–235.

Arlen, M. *The View from Highway 1: Essays on Television.* New York: Farrar, Straus & Giroux, 1976.

Auletta, K. "Fourteen Truisms for the Communications Revolution." *Media Studies Journal* 10:2–3 (Spring-Summer 1996): 29–38.

Bagdikian, B.H. *The Media Monopoly.* (2nd ed.) Boston: Beacon Press, 1987.

Baker, W.F., & Dessart, G. *Down the Tube: An Inside Account of the Failure of American Television.* New York: Basic Books, 1998.

Bambrough, R. "Aristotle on Justice: A Paradigm of Philosophy." In *New Essays on Plato and Aristotle,* edited by R. Bambrough. London: Routledge & Kegan Paul, 1965.

Barber, B.R. *Jihad vs. McWorld.* New York: Ballantine Books, 1995.

———. *A Passion for Democracy: American Essays.* Princeton, NJ, Princeton University Press, 1998.

Barnouw, E., et al., eds. *Conglomerates and the Media.* New York: The New Press, 1997.

Basseches, M. *Dialectical Thinking and Adult Development.* Norwood, NJ: Ablex Publishing Co., 1984.

Bennett, D.H. *The Party of Fear: From Nativist Movements to the New Right in American History.* (2nd ed.) New York: Vintage Books, 1995.

Berlin, I. *The Hedgehog and the Fox.* Chicago: Ivan R. Dee, 1993.

Bobbio, N. *Left and Right: The Significance of a Political Distinction.* Chicago: U. of Chicago Press, 1996.

Borgmann, A. "The Moral Assessment of Technology." In *Democracy in a Technological Society,* edited by L. Winner. Dordrecht: Kluwer Publishers, 1992.

Bourdieu, P. *On Television.* New York: The New Press, 1998.

Bullert, B.J. *Public Television: Politics and the Battle Over Documentary Film.* New Brunswick, NJ: Rutgers U. Press, 1997.

Casti, J.L. *Complexification: Explaining a Paradoxical World Through the Science of Surprise.* New York: HarperCollins, 1994.

Conrad, P. *Television: The Medium and Its Manners.* London: Routledge & Kegan Paul, 1983.

Dionne, E.J., Jr. *They Only Look Dead: Why Progressives Will Dominate the Next Political Era.* New York: Simon & Schuster, 1996.

Durgnat, R. "Mind's Eye, Eye's Mind: Transformation by Context." *Quarterly Review of Film Studies* 9:2 (Spring 1984): 89–100.

Fallows, J. *Breaking the News: How the Media Undermine American Democracy.* New York: Pantheon Books, 1996.

Funkhouser, G.R., & Shaw, E.F. "How Synthetic Experience Shapes Social Reality." *Journal of Communication* 40:2 (Spring 1990): 75–87.

Gans, H. "Varieties of American Political Spectra." *Social Research* 60:3 (Fall 1993): 513–529.

Gerbner, G. "Television: The New State Religion?" *Et cetera* 34:2 (June 1977): 145–150.

Gibson, W. "Network News: Elements of a Theory." *Social Text* 2:3 (Fall 1980): 88–111.

Gitlin, T. "Television's Anti-politics: Surveying the Wasteland." *Dissent* (Winter 1996): 76–85.

——. "Blips, Bites and Savvy Talk: Television's Impact on American Politics." *Dissent* (Winter 1990): 18–26.

——. (ed.) *Watching Television*. New York: Pantheon Books, 1986.

——. *Inside Prime Time*. New York: Pantheon Books, 1985.

——. "Sixteen Notes on Television and the Movement." In *Literature in Revolution*, edited by G.A. White and C. Newman. New York: Holt, Rinehard and Winston, 1972.

Glasser, I. "Television and the Construction of Reality." *Et cetera* 45:2 (Summer 1988): 156–162.

Gopnik, A. "A Critic at Large: Read All About It." *The New Yorker*, Dec. 12, 1994.

Green, P. "American Television and Consumer Democracy." *Dissent* (Spring 1998): 49–57.

Greider, W. *Who Will Tell the People: The Betrayal of American Democracy*. New York: Simon & Schuster, 1992.

Hallin, D.C. "The American News Media: A Critical Theory Perspective." In *Critical Theory and Public Life*, edited by J. Forester. Cambridge, MA: MIT Press, 1985.

Hart, R. *Seducing America: How Television Charms the Modern Voter*. New York: Oxford University Press, 1994.

Hertsgaard, M. *On Bended Knee: The Press and the Reagan Presidency*. New York: Farrar, Straus & Giroux, 1988; Schocken Books, 1989.

Hirschman, A.O. *The Rhetoric of Reaction*. Cambridge, MA: Harvard U. Press, 1991.

Hodgson, G. *The World Turned Right Side Up: A History of the Conservative Ascendancy in America*. New York: Houghton Mifflin, 1996.

Hughes, R. *The Culture of Complaint*. New York: Warner Books, 1993.

Huston, A., et al. *Big World, Small Screen: The Role of Television in American Society*. (Task force of the American Psychological Association). Lincoln, NE: U. of Nebraska Press, 1992.

Iyengar, S. *Is Anyone Responsible?: How Television Frames Political Issues*. Chicago and London: U. of Chicago Press, 1991.

Jamieson, K.H. *Dirty Politics: Deception, Distraction, and Democracy*. New York: Oxford University Press, 1992.

Jervis, R. *System Effects: Complexity in Political and Social Life*. Princeton, NJ: Princeton U. Press, 1997.

Kaplan, E.A., ed., *Regarding Television: Critical Approaches*. Frederick, MD: University Publications of America, 1983.

Knight, G. "The Reality Effects of Tabloid Television News" in M. Raboy & P. A. Bruck, eds., *Communication For and Against Democracy*. Montreal & New York: Black Rose Books, 1989.

Kurtz, H. *Hot Air: All Talk, All the Time*. New York: Times Books, 1996.

Langsdorf, L. "Dialogue, Distanciation, and Engagement: Toward a Logic of Televisual Communication." *Informal Logic* 10:3 (Fall 1988): 151–168.

"Is Critical Thinking a Technique, or a Means of Enlightenment?" *Informal Logic* 8 (Winter 1986): 1–17.

Lasch, C. *The Revolt of the Elites and the Betrayal of Democracy*. New York: W.W. Norton, 1995.

Ledbetter, J. *Made Possible By . . . : The Death of Public Broadcasting in the United States*. New York: Verso, 1997.

McChesney, R.W. *Corporate Media and the Threat to Democracy*. New York: Seven Stories Press, 1997.

Mander, J. *Four Arguments for the Elimination of Television*. New York: Quill, 1978.

Marlow, E. "Media and Culture." *Et cetera* 50:3 (Fall 1993): 296–309.

Meyrowitz, J. "Understandings of Media." *Et cetera* 56:1 (Spring 1999): 44–52.

——. "Multiple Media Literacies." *Journal of Communication* 48:1 (Winter 1998): 96–108.

——. *No Sense of Place: The Impact of Electronic Media on Social Behavior*. New York: Oxford University Press, 1985.

Miller, M.C. *Boxed In: The Culture of TV*. Evanston, IL: Northwestern U. Press, 1988.

Pichel, I. "Seeing with the Camera." *Hollywood Quarterly* Vol. 1 (1945–46): 138–145.

Postman, N. "The Information Environment." *Et cetera* 36:3 (Fall 1979): 234–245.

———. "Critical Thinking in the Electronic Era." *National Forum* 65 (Winter 1985): 4–8, 17.

———. *Amusing Ourselves to Death: Public Discourse in the Age of Show Business*. New York: Viking Penguin, 1985.

Ranney, A. *Channels of Power: The Impact of Television on American Politics*. New York: Basic Books, 1983.

Robinson, G.J. "Television News and the Claim to Facticity." In *Interpreting Television: Current Research Perspectives*, edited by W.D. Rowland, Jr., & B. Watkins. Beverly Hills, CA: Sage, 1984.

Sabato, L.J. *Feeding Frenzy: How Attack Journalism has Transformed American Politics*. New York: The Free Press, 1991.

Schechter, D. *The More You Watch the Less You Know: News Wars/(Sub) Merged Hopes/Media Adventures*. New York: Seven Stories Press, 1997.

Sclove, R.E. *Democracy and Technology*. New York: Guilford Press, 1995.

Sontag, S. *On Photography*. New York: Farrar, Straus & Giroux, 1977.

Sowell, T. A. *Conflict of Visions: Ideological Origins of Political Struggles*. New York: William Morrow, 1987.

Stadler, H. "The Spectacle of Theory: An Historical Speculation." *Wide Angle* 8:1 (1986): 4–9.

Starobin, P. "A Generation of Vipers: Journalists and the New Cynicism" *Columbia Journalism Review* (Mar/Apr.1995): 25–32.

Stephens, M. "Deconstruction and the Get-Real Press." *Columbia Journalism Review* (Sept.-Oct. 1991): 38–42.

Walzer, M. *Spheres of Justice: A Defense of Pluralism and Equality*. New York: Basic Books, 1983.

———. *On Toleration*. New Haven, CT: Yale University Press, 1997.
Winn, M. *The Plug-In Drug: Television, Children, and the Family*. (Revised ed.) New York: Penguin Books, 1985.